PLEASE HELP ME
DO IT MYSELF

*OBSERVATION AND RECORDKEEPING
FOR THE MONTESSORI PRIMARY
AND ELEMENTARY CLASS*

SUSAN MAYCLIN STEPHENSON

II

Other books in this series

*The Joyful Child: Montessori, Global Wisdom
for Birth to Three*

*Child of the World: Montessori, Global Education
for Age 3-12+*

The Red Corolla, Montessori Cosmic Education (for age 3-6)

The Universal Child, Guided by Nature

Montessori and Mindfulness

No Checkmate, Montessori Chess Lessons for Age 3-90+

Montessori Homeschooling, One Family's Story

Aid to Life, Montessori Beyond the Classroom

PLEASE HELP ME DO IT MYSELF
Observation and Recordkeeping for the
Montessori Primary and Elementary Class

Copyright © 2022 Susan Mayclin Stephenson
www.susanart.net

Michael Olaf Montessori Company
PO Box 1162
Arcata, CA 95518, USA
www.michaelolaf.net
michaelolafcompany@gmail.com

For translation and foreign publishing rights contact:
michaelolafbooks@gmail.com

ISBN 978-1-879264-28-1

Cover: painting "Concentration" by the author
More information: www.susanart.net
Illustrations: by the author

CONTENTS

THE ELEMENTARY CLASS, Ages 6 to 12

FINAL CHAPTERS

PREFACE

A friend gave me a book, *The Montessori Method,* by Maria Montessori, when I was in graduate school. Reading it inspired me to put our first child in a Montessori school in San Francisco, California, and the changes in her were dramatic. They were very much in line about what one might expect in a true Montessori experience. It seemed that learning to be this kind of teacher was more valuable than continuing graduate school, so I asked the head of the school the best place to learn to teach like this.

She told me: "If you can manage it, study at the AMI training center in London that was begun by Dr. Montessori's son, Mario Montessori." My first Montessori teacher training course was the 58th being held in London, so there had been fifty-seven courses held previously, the lecturers learning from the students during each course, just as any teacher learns from students.

Over the years I have worked with teachers in many countries who have taken the same kind of training as I, but, also, I worked with teachers following many other kinds of Montessori teacher training, and some who are only able to learn about Montessori from reading a book. The difference in the results in classrooms is varied.

As one example, years ago, there was an article in a Montessori newsletter reporting on the progress of Montessori in several of the first Montessori in public-school experiments. I will never forget the words of one principal: "Finally we have two completely outfitted Montessori environments, and next year we hope to find a trained Montessori teacher."

The focus on materials, rather than on teacher training and some kind of deep understanding of Montessori, is something one sees everywhere today. It is a sign of our times, *buying* rather than *doing*, and looking for a quick solution.

However, there can also be positive results following only a beginning understanding of Montessori philosophy. For example, one day I was visiting a traditional school in Asia where the teachers were trying to transition to being a Montessori school. Observing absolutely no sign of anything you or I would consider a Montessori environment or Montessori practice, it was explained to me that, at this school, corporal punishment was not used to exact discipline. This was what had been gleaned from their first introduction to Montessori, a radical idea for this time and place, and a good place to begin.

In the beginning of her work Montessori encouraged many of her students to train others to become teachers. But very quickly it became evident that many of the results of this secondary training were not successful. So why was that?

Montessori was a scientist, skilled at observation, data analysis, strategic planning, and standard scientific research. She spent thousands of daytime hours observing the children in the first Montessori class in Rome. At night, she studied her notes and came up with ideas of what to do next.

There was clearly a need for a program whereby teachers could gain the skills to become successful teacher trainers. So, in 1929 Montessori formed the Association Montessori Internationale, or AMI. For almost 100 years now this organization has maintained a high standard of teacher training, and developed other ways to help children and adults all over the world, and in many situations. Under this kind of teacher training one learns to observe without judgement, to keep records, to analyze the data, and to come up with a plan, and then to continue this cycle of education by "following the child."

Here are a few details of an AMI primary teacher training course. Unless the course is part of an undergraduate university degree, a university degree is required. A diploma course includes, but is not limited to: (1) 120 lecture hours; (2) 140 hours of practice with the materials supervised by staff, this means giving lessons to other adults (not practicing lessons on children); (3) a minimum of 90 hours of observation in an approved classroom; (4) a minimum of 80 hours of teaching practice in an approved classroom; (5) passing the oral and written exams.

Here are some details of the program of becoming an AMI teacher trainer: (1) passing the exams of an AMI course, for example 0-3, 3-6, or 6-12; (2) a minimum of five years full-time successful teaching at that level; (3) participating full time in three AMI courses at that level, during which time the trainer-in-training gradually learns to carry out all of the elements of a teacher training course; (4) research papers; (5) giving several introduction, or orientation, courses at that level; (6) acceptance as a teacher trainer.

Montessori in a Nutshell

Over the years many of us have been asked to explain Montessori in a Nutshell, or in a very few words. Here is one of my own attempts:

> *When Montessori practice is authentic, a child (or adult) will experience many opportunities of deep concentration on activities that are appropriate for that person's stage of development, activities that have been demonstrated carefully, and then chosen by the child. Such deep involvement while carrying out meaningful activities, over a period of time, will eventually lead to the transformation of the person's personality, exhibiting calm and more orderly behaviour, greater interest in constructive activities and work and study, kindness, cooperation, affection, greater social awareness, and the development of inner discipline.*

The mastery of academic or other life skills, for which Montessori education is so famous, is a natural outcome when the inner guide of each human is in charge of the path, and the work enjoyed is also remembered.

What are these activities that can bring about the transformation? It is the purpose of Montessori training, and years of careful observation, record-keeping, exploring the data, making plans, and then more observation, to be skilled at learning to carry out, and then presenting these activities, at just the right moment.

This book contains some of the ways that I have used observation and record keeping just for this purpose.

I know that many people reading this book will not have had the kind of teacher training that I was fortunate to receive. Please do not despair. You are not alone. Understanding Montessori can be a lifetime of discovery. Each time we use our developing skill to observe a child we learn something new. Each time we open a book written by Montessori we discover something new because we ourselves are changing constantly. Even after fifty years I am amazed at how much there is to learn and how enjoyable this kind of learning can be.

GENERAL INTRODUCTION

Human beings are born with a drive to observe, explore, and understand. We can see in the facial expressions and actions, of even the youngest child, a natural curiosity about the real world, the home, and the classroom, both inside and outside. In the first years there is a desire to touch, smell, taste, manipulate, and understand this world. The foundational knowledge of the immediate world, and of one's own interaction and abilities in this world, is laid down in the first six years.

In the elementary years, age six through twelve, and beyond, this sense of wonder is closer to astonishment as one becomes aware of being a part of something larger than oneself. There is a desire to understand the history and reality of the world's greatness, and to explore how one might participate in this greatness. At this age, one tends to ask the Great Questions of the Heart: who am I, where did we come from? why are we here? how and what do I like to learn? what makes happiness? how do humans best relate to other humans? why is there war? are animals persons? why do people get angry? what happens to us after death? and more.

These questions form the beginning of the deep part of the field of philosophy. It is the consideration of the need to search for the answers of these questions, rather than any academic brilliance, that should remain the central focus in Montessori.

Dr. Maria Montessori was an active and dedicated supporter of women's rights and peace movements. After witnessing the unexpected and extremely positive response of children to her methods, she realized the potential of this kind of education as a way to completely reshape society, not through any imposition of academic requirements upon children, but by supporting the development of the mind, body, and spirit of each child's unique potential and development.

In Montessori education, the teacher learns to meld the theory and the practice, the esoteric and the practical, in a process that is ongoing. The teacher is first of all an observer; then, when skilled in recognizing stages of development and individual needs, the facilitator of further exploration.

Sometimes the Montessori classroom teacher is called a *director* or *directress*, or a *guide*. But the word *teacher* is also appropriate when the definition is a person who helps another acquire knowledge, competence, or virtue. Personally, I think of myself, when working with either children or adults, as a *door opener*. One of the joys of teaching is the opening of a door to new information and experiences. The teacher, may decide which doors to offer, this decision based observation. But it works best when the student decides which door to walk through. I do not want to direct, or guide, a person to a particular end, or down a predetermined path, but to help each reach their individually chosen goal.

The beginning and end of each day in a Montessori primary or elementary class is unique. No matter what we might have planned as far as lessons for a new day, it is part of the thrill of teaching Montessori that we had no idea, as we look back on the day's work, where the exploration will have taken each child, or a group of children.

The only thing that we know for sure is that for any age—from birth to the elderly—deep concentration on appropriate work that is self-chosen, and protected from interruption, is a gift to be cherished. Such periods of meditation-like concentration feed the body, mind, and soul of an individual. In an environment with adults who support this kind of education, the activities can develop a myriad of physical and mental skills and abilities, provide time for exploring the great questions, and reveal positive characteristics of the human, including the compassionate instincts that follow deep concentration.

One of Montessori's first discoveries of this inborn potential is shared in the chapter "My Contribution to Experimental Science" from *The Advanced Montessori Method, Volume One*:

> *I happened to notice a little girl of about three years old deeply absorbed in a set of solid insets, removing the wooden cylinders from their respective holes and replacing them. The expression on the child's face was one of such concentrated attention that it seemed to me an extraordinary manifestation; up to this time none of the children had ever shown such fixity of interest in an object; and my belief in the characteristic instability of attention in young children, who flit incessantly from one thing to another, made me peculiarly alive to the phenomenon. I watched the child intently without disturbing her at first, and began to count how many times she repeated the exercises; then, seeing that she was continuing for a long time, I picked up the little armchair in which she was seated, and placed chair and child upon the table; the little creature hastily caught up her case of insets, laid it across the arms of her chair, and gathering the cylinders into her lap, set to work again. Then I called*

upon all the children to sing; they sang, but the little girl continued undisturbed, repeating her exercise even after the short song had come to an end. I counted forty-four repetitions; when at last she ceased, it was quite independently of any surrounding stimuli which might have distracted her, and she looked round with a satisfied air, almost as if awaking from a refreshing nap.

This phenomenon gradually became common among the children. And each time such a polarization of attention took place, the child began to be completely transformed, to become calmer, more intelligent, and more expansive; it showed extraordinary spiritual qualities, recalling the phenomena of a higher consciousness.

When the phenomenon of the polarization of attention had taken place, all that was disorderly and fluctuating in the consciousness of the child seemed to be organizing itself into a spiritual creation, the surprising characteristics of which are reproduced in every individual. It made me think of the life of man which may remain diffused among a multiplicity of things, in an inferior state of chaos, until some special thing attracts it intensely and fixes it; and then man is revealed unto himself, he feels that he has begun to live.

In the beginning of a teaching career one might feel that observation is a tedious requirement, and we might find reasons to avoid this part of our work; after all, there is a lot to do. But when one begins to carry out detailed observations regularly, the results show that observation is not only necessary, but it has the potential to provide a path to greater happiness for all.

As we learn to observe children, we begin to observe ourselves while interacting with them. We begin to pay attention to our own words and actions, and our relationships with others. As we learn to schedule time to step back, to be in the moment, to observe without judgment, we learn more about ourselves, who we are and what we need. And, in the Montessori classroom, this is how we learn to meet the needs of our students.

The details of observation and record keeping that I share in this book, have worked for me over the years, and I have shared some of them with both traditional and Montessori teachers, and with parents. These are just my own methods and there are many others. Please take what is helpful to you, and adapt to fit your own situation. Just as each child follows a unique path in the work in the Montessori environment, each adult must find a way of being, and of helping children, that matches each personality and way of working.

No matter what your Montessori teacher training or parenting practices may be, I hope you will find something in the following pages that will support you in your most important task, that is bringing forth the very best in human beings.

PRIMARY CLASS INTRODUCTION

For age six and older, in most places, there are academic requirements. But in the Montessori infant community (age 1-2.5 year) and primary class (age 2.5-6 years) there are no academic requirements. Everything is offered, and the choice of work is up to the child.

One year, as I was giving a workshop on primary materials and lessons in Thailand, we began to discuss the importance of keeping track of all of the lessons in all of the areas of work, for the purpose of recordkeeping. One of the teachers asked me how many pieces of materials, and how many lessons there are in a primary class. I didn't have a number, but the group of teachers had their primary albums with them so I suggested they count. One student counted 300, another with 400.

There is much more to observe and keep records of than materials and lessons. We observe the environment and what materials are being chosen and which are not; we observe the interactions of the children; we observe our own thoughts and feelings and responses to various situations; we observe why it appears that a child might choose an activity that is not a challenge; was the task carried through to the end or not completed, and so much more.

But at the basis of all, we observe the level of concentration on an activity, because it is this deep concentration that is most important in our work. For each child, there is an event called "the polarization of attention." This term describes an event, when a child is carrying out of an activity, and for the first time this task engages the child completely.

Such a polarization of attention occurs in a Montessori class because (1) the teacher offers a child new to the class several lessons on basic materials, (2) the child has "tasted" these choices, and then gradually begins to make wise choices of what to work on, and (3) one day one of these choices turns out to be just what the child needed at that moment.

Usually a child experiencing this miracle will continue to work, completely unaware of what is going on in the room, for a long time. In modern terms, we might call this the experience of *mindfulness* or even *meditation*. The child is different from that moment on, clearly looking for other activities that will provide the same experience. Experience that enables the mind and the body to work together for the same purpose; this results in happiness.

In order for our children to reach this point, it is necessary for the teacher to be skilled in many ways: preparing the environment and the materials, practicing giving the lessons to another adult, observing and recordkeeping of the work and progress in concentration of each child.

Materials and Lessons in the Primary Class

In deciding what materials to have in the classroom, there are several things to consider.

(1) Is the material a "key"? A key opens a door and only one key is necessary. We should not waste a child's precious energy on duplication and confusion. For example, there should be only one set of materials that give practice honing the skill of determining the difference between *loud* and *soft*, *louder* and *softer*, *loudest* and *softest*, leaned through repeated practice pairing and grading the *sound boxes*. There should be only one exercise to teach how to form, to write, the symbols of 1-10, the *sandpaper numbers*. And so on. The child then learns that every single activity in the classroom is important and interesting, that each one has one purpose, something unique and special to discover.

(2) How long does the activity take and does it lead to repetition? Sometimes activities that are not taught in a teacher training course are found in the classroom. Usually they have no realistic purpose, often take only a moment, and so do not require much in terms as concentration, and do not offer a skill to be mastered. The many "transfer" activities that I often find in classrooms are an example of this "busy work."

(3) Are the materials beautiful and in perfect condition? Wood, glass, other non-plastic materials inspire children as well as adults to want to handle materials and to treat them with respect. Are they kept clean and in good repair so they can fulfill their purpose? This is important in attracting children to take an active part in learning instead of a passive one.

(4) Does each piece of material have its place on the shelf or in the environment? When a child has a sudden inspiration to polish shoes for example, it should be easy to find the necessary materials in the expected place, ready to use.

(5) Are the materials being used correctly? If the teacher understands exactly what the purpose is, what is to be learned, what concept abstracted, it will be clear when a piece of material is being helpful, fulfilling the aim of that material, or is being misused. For example, a paint brush should not be used to stir soup. One of the number rods should not be used to hammer a nail. The cubes of the pink tower should not be used as building blocks to create forts and castles. Sometimes "follow the child" is misinterpreted to mean that anything a child does with the materials is valid work and should be allowed. This is clearly not the case.

If the lesson does not "open a door" to a new concept and skill, and if it does not lead to the mastery of further work, it probably should not be in the classroom. The wise teacher is quick to kindly stop any mis-use of materials, but in a positive way. For example, explaining to the child as the mis-use is stopped, "Oh, I forgot, I have to take this material out of the classroom for a bit. Don't worry it will be back soon."

Many years have gone into the development of the materials and lessons which call the child to involvement, concentration, and mastery. Here is a short overview of each area.

Practical Life materials and lessons

These lessons give specific tools for learning to control one's body (walking on the line), caring for oneself (dressing frames, brushing teeth, etc.), caring for all of the materials in the classroom beginning with those in the cultural areas such as handling water, caring for plants and animals, handling musical instruments correctly, and so on.

All of these lessons should reflect what a child has grown up observing in the home. Good manners, or the grace and courtesy lessons, are also specific to the culture. They enable a child to give to others, such as serving food to friends, or helping to tie a shoe or an apron. And they provide practice in skills, such as handing an object to another person, or moving around a friend's floor mat so as to not interrupt work, that helps a child feel confident in the company of others.

The Cultural materials and lessons

Rather than taking children at this age out into the world for field trips, the "world" is brought into the classroom, by means of materials and activities in the following areas: physics, botany, zoology, history, geography, music, and art. Each area has corresponding practical life and sensorial and language elements. And they often enable us adults to keep learning along with the children.

After delivering the lectures in this area for the first AMI primary diploma course in Morocco, I presented them in the book: *The Red Corolla, Montessori Cosmic Education* (for age 3-6).

The Sensorial materials and lessons

These materials and lessons open the child's mind to the world. It makes one aware of colors, shapes, textures, sounds, tastes, weight. The more the child works with these materials the more refined become the abilities to distinguish variations. This is the material that teaches the fine details of movement that was learned in the practical life work. Perceptions of the world, and one's own efforts in careful movement are more challenging, more interesting.

Language materials and lessons

Language is connected to all of the other areas of the classroom. The adult, as model and as listener, is the most important language "material" at this age. Because this is the time when children need to move and to touch in order to learn, language is taught through movement such as the sandpaper letters and movable alphabet.

When they are able to attend a Montessori primary class for the entire multi-year cycle, most children learn first to write and later to read. They explore the meaning and use of words, sentences, paragraphs, indexes, look for information in books, write stories, etc. But learning to read and write is not the main goal and is not the case for each child.

What is most important is that children are listened to with our complete attention so they have a desire to communicate; they are allowed to speak and ask questions; they are read to, and see others reading books; they see parents, teachers, other adults, and their classmates writing and reading; they observe daily that these activities are enjoyable.

Math materials and lessons

As you read this do you cringe? My father was a physicist and loved math. He tried to talk to me about the excitement of using a slide rule (an early computer) and didn't understand why I didn't love math as he did. But my own math memories revolved around the stress of being tested on multiplication tables.

The materials and lessons in the Montessori primary class, above all, teach that math can be beautiful and enjoyable. Even if a particular area of math is not something one child chooses to spend time on, they will see all of the math materials being enjoyed by someone, some time. This is a gift to all.

These lessons give the child an introduction to concepts in a sensorial way that may stay throughout life. These include learning to count up to 1,000 by handling beads and other materials; feeling in one's hands and seeing with one's eyes the difference between a unit, ten, hundred, thousand, and a half, quarter, tenth, and so on. Being given specific lessons on how to sensorially explore addition, subtraction, multiplication, division, and fractions helps a person make sense of these skills later, when they are abstractions. Even memorization of the multiplication tables occurs naturally during this absorbent mind period of human development

Reading, writing, 'rithmetic

Even though Montessori preschools are sometimes famous above all for early reading, writing, and math, I hope this chapter is successful in helping to explain how these subjects are approached and taught. As with all of the work at this age, the goal of providing a sensorial introduction to language and math and geometry is to provide enjoyment, to inspire curiosity, and to do this through materials that can be enjoyed for long periods of time and with deep concentration which is the essence of Montessori in any area and at any age.

Typical Day Schedule

In order to keep deep concentration at the center of our work, the uninterrupted minimum three-hour work period each morning, and at least two-hour work period in the afternoon, should be the first consideration. For the most part, traditional preschool events such as circle time, whole group activities, or as Montessori refers to them, collective lessons, do not have a place in an authentic Montessori primary class. An experienced teacher develops, over time, the ability to observe all of the children in the class while, at the same time, giving a lesson to an individual child. Such a teacher knows when to step in, when to offer a lesson, when to collect a few unfocused children for a spontaneous small group activity.

However, in times of stress it is often the case that this teacher, if their own education was in a traditional teacher-directed education, might fall back on this traditional experience in order to cope. For example, the teacher might tend to move away from the Montessori training, to give constant collective lessons, a have a teacher's desk, to impose silence, to tell the children what to work on and give assignments, and so forth. Keeping a teacher's journal, discussed later, can be a kind of self-talk to get one back on track.

It always helps me to remember that Maria Montessori used the name *casa dei bambini*, which means a children's *house*, not children's *school*. This should be a place where one's needs can be met if one is tired, hungry, overwhelmed and in need of a little space off in the book corner, or a walk outside. And it is the place where one is offered a myriad of exciting and satisfying activities geared to individual needs and interests, and where one's deep concentration on these activities is protected from interruption. It is valuable to think of our environments as homes, and the students as honored guests. And the schedule as one that we would follow with our guests.

Of course, there are clear limits. Lunch is sometimes cooked and hot at a certain time. Drop-off and pick-up time is scheduled. And there are some basic limits in how the class operates. All of these lessons are taught, following the dictate "Teach by teaching, not by correcting."

1 – The children learn, through little courtesy lessons, to respect and not interrupt one who is focused on an activity.

2 – They learn how to care for and respect the environment and colleagues, and to use the materials in such a way that the aim, the purpose, of materials is being followed, helping them to grow in understanding.

3 – The children learn that they can work on anything if they understand the purpose, and use the materials in the way they are intended to help them learn.

4 – They learn to put their work back when finished, all in order and ready for a friend to choose.

For the rest of the day, the schedule is dictated by the children as they carry out daily life in their Montessori home.

An Error and an Experiment

My first year of teaching was at a large school in San Francisco, in 1971. It was recommended by our well-trained and experienced head teacher that I have a long group lesson at the beginning or end of every morning. I was new and she was experienced, so even though I did not learn to do this in my teacher training in London, I followed her advice.

I had already learned how important it is to allow a child, who already has a work goal in mind, to come into the classroom in the morning and get right to work. So, I chose to have my group lesson at the end of the morning. I knew that a three-hour work period was important so I had as short a group lesson as possible, but never did I feel that it met the needs of a group of children from 2.5 to 6.5 years of age. There was always someone who was bored and fidgety.

In every other area, I was doing what I had learned during my training, but saw no great concentration and normalization like that I had seen during observations and student teaching in London, or read about in Montessori's books. Instead of two or three activities involving deep concentration in a morning, the children were spending short periods of time on many activities. This was not good.

Finally, an AMI consultant, Margot Waltuch who had worked with Montessori for many years, came as my primary consultant. She was very impressed with the independence of the work of the class until it came time for the end of the morning group activity. I gathered all of the children into a group and began a song.

Here are her words: "Did you learn to do this during your training?"

"No," I replied, and began to explain about the master teacher.

Then she said, "What is this mother hen and chicks phenomenon I see all over the United States!"

I was so relieved! That was my last group lesson in the primary teaching years, and it helped me develop ways to avoid group lessons later, as a 6-12 teacher.

A work-period experiment

Because I had a group of families very interested in learning about Montessori, which I shared with them through regular newsletters that formed the basis for my later books, they supported my experiment.

The old schedule:

Arrival 8:30-9 (no entering the class after 9)

Uninterrupted work period until noon. A three-hour+ work period

Lunch (no cooking was allowed so children brought their lunch in a lunch box) 12-1

Work period from 1-3

Departure from 3-3:30 (from the outside garden in good weather)

19

The new schedule:

Arrival 8:30-9

Departure 2-2:30

So, we went from a three-hour work period to a five-hour work period, 9am to 2pm, with no lunch break. It was even a potential six-hour work period for a child who arrived at 8:30 and left at 2:30!

At any time between 8:30 and 2:30 a child could set a table and unpack and eat their food from home. They could rest or sleep on a floor mat. There was not direct access to the outside area but there were three "outside" tickets that any child, or two or three children together, could pin on their clothing and go out. I could see them from the classroom window.

Experiment Results

What I learned was, just as a wider age range creates a much higher level of independence and work mastery, the longer the uninterrupted work period — or in today's language the longer the child was allowed to be in "flow" — the deeper the concentration, the more successful the work, the more challenging the attempted work, the happier the children, and the more rested they are at the end of the day.

School Consultant Returns

The next time Mrs. Waltuch came to be my official AMI consultant, we watched the children, with no adults in the room, through a one-way mirror. They went on with their work calmly and independently, unaware of us.

Margot said, mightily pleased, "The children don't seem to miss you." I was pleased too.

Conclusion

20

This success was not just because of the great age span and long work period. It depended on meticulous observation and recordkeeping. There is a great difference between being busy and being engaged.

Hopefully the following chapters — explaining the concentration graphs, the weekly lesson plan, the mastery charts, and the teachers journal — will help make following Montessori ideas easier and more successful wherever they are being implemented.

SUPPORTING CONCENTRATION

In order to succeed in our work, we need to have a sound knowledge of both Montessori theory and practice. And above all we need to have the ability to observe and understand the child. Why did Montessori place such emphasis on observation? She considered it to be an integral and continuous cornerstone of the adult's work. It is the indispensable part which makes our work meaningful. It allows us to truly follow the child, and to continually refine and improve our own understanding and ability.

In the following chapters of this book there are other important tools for observation, but at the core, as you will read later, are what Montessori called work curves, and I refer to as concentration graphs. As you will see presented in these graphs shown later in this chapter, there are stages a child goes through on the path to inner development and happiness through concentration. They could be briefly described as follows:

First, the child cannot concentrate or work on anything for long even though the teacher has presented work that is appropriate to the child's stage of development. There could also be disorderly and disruptive periods.

Next, the child begins to get involved with activities he has been shown and begins to concentrate for very short periods of time. These periods are often followed by periods of restlessness, watching others, touching materials. At this stage, there is then often an activity chosen into which the child can put some effort, and experience slightly deeper concentration. At this stage, the child may experience a period of rest as the work is being processed in the brain. This period of rest should not be interrupted.

Eventually the child is able to concentrate for longer periods and the following periods of restlessness disappear. The child goes more directly from one activity to the next, easily choosing appropriate work. Often the morning of a child at this stage ends in contemplation, again, not to be interrupted.

Finally, this child sometimes enters the classroom having already decided what to work on. This is an elevation of inner direction, the goal throughout all Montessori education at any age. The main characteristics of a child at this age are perseverance, calmness, inner discipline.

Lessons/Presentations

The children are free to choose the exercises they prefer; but of course, as the teacher initiates them in each exercise, they only choose the objects they know how to use. The teacher, observing them, sees when the child is sufficiently natured for more advanced exercises, and introduces them, or perhaps the child begins them after watching other children more advanced.

—Montessori, *The Advanced Montessori Method, I*

It is a great skill to be able to look at a child, consider what sensitive period might be being manifest (language, movement, order, interest in small things, etc.), what abilities the child has, and which ones need practice, or what the child is closely observing others working on. If we notice that a child is having trouble holding a pencil correctly we do not correct, but offer a new lesson on materials with knobs such as the cylinder blocks or puzzle maps. Trying to communicate unsuccessfully about sensorial quality? We offer a three-period lesson with the appropriate sensorial material. And because of having had many hours of presenting materials to other adults during training, these lessons are at our fingertips, not just in our albums, folders, our brains.

Choosing Work

The adult keeps careful track of what lessons a child is ready for and can come up with others to offer on the spur of the moment. But there are two sentences that I hope you never hear an adult utter in your classroom.

The first one is, "You need to find something to do." Hearing these words, a child will almost always choose "busywork," something that does NOT fulfill a need! It will be something easy and meaningless, and sadly results in the experience of being bored while moving one's hands and pretending to work, the opposite of what we hope for a child.

The other is, "You are not ready for that work yet." At this age, a child does not have a concept of the difference between the present and the future as far as thinking about capabilities. The child, in this instance, probably hears, "You are not ready for this work and never will be."

I remember, in my primary classes, the attraction of very young children to the advanced, beautiful long chains and squares and cubes in the math area. If this attraction was more than casual I would ask, "Would you like to dust this math material?" Then I would give a clear lesson on just how to do this. Another way to allow children with a deep interest in an area of the classroom that is appropriate for older children is to show a young child how to lay out a floor mat next to a shelf of more advanced materials, carefully remove all of the material from one shelf one piece at a time, starting from the left side of the shelf, and lay it out in the exact order as on the shelf. Then to dust the entire shelf, and each piece of material as it is carefully replaced on the shelf.

Contemplation as Work

Children are given lessons in the form of play-acting on how to watch a person work without interrupting. And how to wait and watch before asking if one child can join another. Much of the courtesy is taught in this way. So, it is fine for this child to think and watch while walking around the room. But it was the children who taught me that it is also fine to do so in the "observer's chair."

My own school in Northern Michigan was in a small community with a junior college. Since ours was one of the very first Montessori schools in the state there was a great interest. Several days a week I had one or two observers from sociology, psychology, or education classes, and even from home economics classes of the high school. In order to not to interrupt the beginning and the ending of the morning these college and high school students (as explained by their professors) arrived mid-morning, entered the classroom quietly, and did not interact with the busy children, as this was considered scientific observation. There were two observers' chairs (the same size as the larger of the children's chairs), each with a clipboard with suggestions for what to look for, and a place for questions. The questions were gathered and answered in a lecture I gave for these college or high school classes at the end of the semester.

The children were taught (by role-playing) to respect the work of the visitor and to not interrupt their important work.

One day I noticed a young boy sitting in an observer's chair; there was a very serious and grown-up look on his face as he watched the other children carry on the morning work. It was clear that he was doing what he had learned a serious scientific observer does. I said nothing, but this official "observing" became another work choice for the children. It was quite successful in many ways. When there were no observing visitors it was considered important "work" for a child to sit and watch the others. It was quite often that after a few minutes, or longer, a child returned to work with great purpose. I am sure that much work was inspired, and concepts learned, by these children's observations.

What Qualifies as Deep Concentration?

"Follow the Child" is a constantly heard sentence in the Montessori world and often misunderstood. It does not mean that everything a child does with the educational materials is valid. The math beads cannot be used to string a necklace. The brown stairs cannot be used as building blocks. Every piece of Montessori didactic material is used in a specific way for good reasons, in order to support the development of the child.

The teacher must try to understand why the child chooses a particular activity, and to understand if it is meeting a physical or mental or emotional need, and then, to carefully observe how involved the child is in this work.

As Montessori says in *The Child in the Family*:

> *Before everything, the* [teacher] *must know how to recognize the phenomenon of the polarization of attention.*

It is clear on the graphs that *contemplation* and *rest* are considered deep concentration or polarization of attention.

I remember a story that Hilla Patel, head of my first Montessori course in London and later director of AMI, told us about a situation in her early years of teaching. A little girl had been sitting on a floor mat in the middle of the room working with the geometric solids. She was through handling the material and just sitting there "doing nothing." Hilla watched and wondered. The girl continued to sit and just look around the room, not moving otherwise. Hilla still watched. Finally, thinking that it was perhaps time to step in and suggest that the little girl do something else, she quietly approached. The girl looked up at Hilla with a face full of wonder and said, "This room is a rectangular prism!"

Hilla pointed out to us that she almost, in her ignorance of what qualifies as deep concentration, destroyed a very important and unique geometric discovery.

When children entered my own primary class for the first time I showed them how to first meet their physical needs; using the bathroom, washing hands, preparing, and eating a little snack, and placing a floor mat in a quiet corner to have rest, and then I moved on to presenting work. At first a new child would choose work because I had offered it. Then choices became more and more based on knowledge of what felt right. Eventually, after a child had experienced the joy of working for long periods of time on work that was exactly suited to the child's interests and stage of development, periods of concentration became longer and deeper. But even then, a child always had the choice to rest, eat, sit, and think, and to observe others, all of these potential experiences in concentration.

There is a lot of evidence to support the value of a child's contemplation in the classroom. We are mistaken in thinking that a child must be constantly doing something with his hands in order to be mindful, concentrating, or to be using his time in what we would consider a valuable way. Even the greatest minds learned that, in creating a great work, no more than a few hours a day was spent actually "on task" and the rest in contemplation of the work. (From "An exploration of the work habits of Darwin, Dickens, Ingmar Bergman, and others"): They only spent a few hours a day doing what we would recognize as their most important work. The rest of the time they were hiking mountains, taking naps, going on walks with friends, or just sitting and thinking. Maybe the key to unlocking the secret of their creativity lies in understanding not just how they labored but how they rested.
– Montessori and Mindfulness

Concentration Graph Examples, including False Fatigue

I found the tracking of depth of concentration during the minimum three-hour morning work period to be the most powerful and useful recordkeeping tool of all. This is a record of the progress in the length of periods of concentration, recorded periodically during the three-hour uninterrupted work periods.

I recorded the graph for one child each day, so that each child was studied several times during the year. Some teachers prefer to record the activity and depth of concentration as a list, to be transferred to the graph at the end of the morning. I found it easier, especially in recording the depth of concentration, to record directly on the graph. After each child had been observed and plotted on a graph, I created one for the entire class.

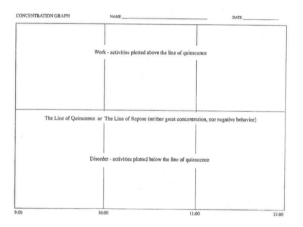

Explanation of concentration graph

This graph is laid out for three hours, from 9:00-12:00 am. The child's name (or "whole class) and the date go at the top. The top line of print explains that a line plotted here is for "Work—activities plotted above the line of quiescence." The middle line explains "The Line of Quiescence" or "The Line of Repose." This means there is neither great concentration, nor negative behavior. This would be the case for any spontaneous small group lesson where deep concentration does not occur. The bottom line of type explains "Disorder—activities plotted below the line of quiescence."

At the very bottom of the graph the hours 9:00, 10:00, 11:00, and 12:00 break the three-hour observation into sections to enable the teacher to plot the levels of concentration. It could be 8:30-11:30 if that fits your schedule. Or 1:00-4:00 if the graph is for the afternoon work period.

Blank graph template

A blank graph is created and copies made for daily use in the classroom. The middle line represents the quiescent state—the child at rest or inactive. The phenomena of order (work) are represented above the line; those of disorder below.

The following graphs are adapted from *The Advanced Montessori Method, Volume One*, the chapter on Experimental Science.

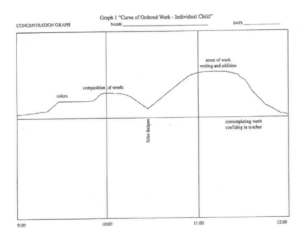

Graph 1 "Curve of Ordered Work - Individual Child"

Graph – curve of ordered work – individual child

This is Montessori's example of a morning of disciplined work:

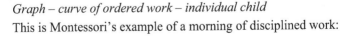

The child keeps still for a while, and then chooses some easy task, such as grading box three of the color

tablets; the child continues working at this for a time, but not for very long; then passes on to some more complicated task, such as that of composing words with the movable letters, and perseveres with this for a long time (about half an hour). At this stage the child ceases working, walks about the room, and appears less calm; to a superficial observer this might seem to be signs of fatigue. But after a few minutes the child undertakes some much more difficult work, and becomes deeply absorbed in this, reaching the acme of the activity (additions and writing down the results). When this work is finished, the activity comes to an end in all serenity; the child contemplates the handiwork for a long time, then approaches the teachers, and begins to confide in her.

When the three-hour uninterrupted cycle is completed the child or the entire class detaches themselves from their internal concentration; they are refreshed and satisfied, experiencing higher social impulses, such as cleaning or organizing the environment, helping, or communicating with others. The appearance of the child in the graph above is that of a person who is rested, satisfied, and uplifted.

False Fatigue

The apparent fatigue of the child in the graph above, between the first and second period of the morning work, is interesting; at that moment, the aspect of the child is not calm and happy as at the end of the morning; indeed, there are seen signs of agitation; the child moves about, and walks, but does not disturb others. It may be said that there is now a search for the maximum satisfaction of interest, and preparation for the "great work" of the morning.

"False Fatigue" is a very important phenomenon to look for and understand. There seems to be a natural rhythm of work, then unrest, then the major or great work of the morning. This mid-morning unrest is a sign for the teacher to step back and let the child or children decide what the major work will be.

NOTE: If the adult steps in at this point and has a group, outside play, snack, etc., the great work will never be seen.

Whole class at work, and false fatigue

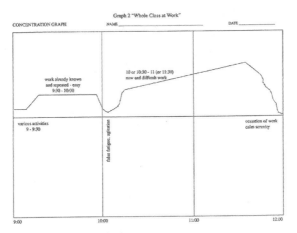

Graph 2 "Whole Class at Work"

Montessori's description:

> *In the first period of the morning, up to about 10 a.m., the occupation chosen is generally an easy and familiar task. At 10 o'clock there is a great commotion; the children are restless, they neither work nor go in quest of materials. The onlooker gets an impression of a tired class, about to become disorderly. After a few minutes, the most perfect order reigns once more; the children are promptly absorbed in work again; they have chosen new and more difficult occupations.*
> *When this work ceases, the children are gentle, calm, and happy.*
>
> *If in the period of 'false fatigue' at 10 a.m. an inexperienced teacher, interpreting the phenomenon of*

suspension or preparation for the culminating work as disorder, intervenes, calling the children to her, and making them rest, etc. their restlessness persists, and the subsequent work is not undertaken. The children do not become calm; they remain in an abnormal state. In other words, if they are interrupted in their cycle, they lose all the characteristics connected with an internal process regularly and completely carried out.

One year a few of us Montessori teachers and trainers were meeting with the government of Sikkim about how they could improve the country's system of education using some Montessori ideas. Jean Miller, AMI Montessori teacher trainer, in explaining the role of the adult during periods similar to false fatigue, "This is the time for the teacher to go make a cup of tea, sit down and wait for the class to settle itself."

NOTE: False Fatigue is often observed in a new child for a period of time, and for the whole class in the beginning of the term or semester. But it disappears as soon as each child becomes self-directed and experiences deep concentration on appropriate work.

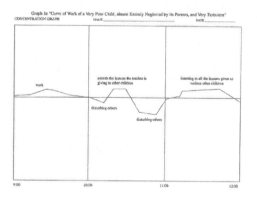

Graph 3a "Curve of Work of a Very Poor Child, almost Entirely Neglected by its Parents, and Very Turbulent"

Curve of work of a child living in poverty, almost entirely neglected by its parents, and very turbulent

This graph is described as that of this child who is probably neglected by parents because they must go to work and the child is left alone, but we see this kind of child today with many other kinds of neglect.

Montessori's description:

> *The child in question seemed to have a tendency to learn from others; [the child] ran away from work or was attracted by it only for a brief moment; and seemed incapable of receiving direct teaching. If any attempt was made to teach something, [the child] grimaced and ran away, wandered about, disturbing companions, and seemed quite intractable; but listened attentively to the lessons the teacher gave to the other children.*

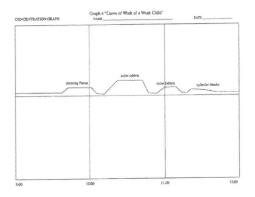

Curve of Work of a Child Advancing Toward Order

Montessori's description:

When [the child] *began to work, after having learned how to do so,* [the child] *persevered, and the normal process is apparent in the diagram; that is to say, preliminary work, a pause (during which the child relapsed slightly and momentarily into the habit of disturbing companions), then the curve of great application, and of final repose (during which however,* [the child] *relapsed into the characteristic defect). The summits of the diagram show not only interest in the work, but a marked kindliness; the child was not only calm, but seemed full of beatitude and gentleness; when at the height of his labors,* [the child] *frequently looked round at companions, and blew little kisses to them on his fingers, but without relaxing attention. It seemed as if a fount of love were gushing up from the fullness of his internal satisfaction, from the depths of a soul that had appeared at first so rough and uncouth.*

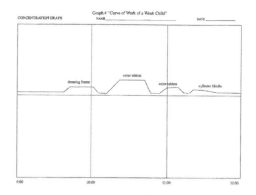

Curve of Work of a Weak Child
Montessori's description:

> *This diagram is made up of curves that fall upon the*
> *line of quiescence; unity of curve is lacking, hence unity of*
> *effort. . . A certain feebleness of character seems to*
> *manifest itself in the halfhearted mental process. The child*
> *makes many successive efforts to rise; but can neither*
> *make the decisive vigorous effort, calm, but this state of*
> *calm has no variations;* [the child] *is neither lively, nor*
> *serene, and not showing strong affectionate impulses.*

In my work consulting with teachers I have seen this often, and here are some of the reasons for the situation:

(1) Too much distraction in the environment, too many materials, visual distraction on the walls, teacher's desk, etc.

(2) Non-Montessori materials which do not lead the child further and deeper into work and concentration. Examples: mindless transferring activities and duplication of "key" materials.

(3) Scheduled interruptions such as specialist teachers, scheduled groups, which teach the child that there is no sense in starting to concentrate because it will be interrupted.

(4) Children not having been taught how to respect the concentration of others, so an attempt at concentration becomes futile.

(5) Too many adults in the environment, so the child is not able to act for himself. Montessori recommended one teacher, and one non-teaching aide for 30-35 children. We often found that the larger the number and the widest the age range, the better, but only if the teacher is prepared.

(6) Incorrect use of materials.

(7) Expectations of how many exercises a child should do in a three-hour period. We look for quality, not quantity, or work.

Course of Progress
Montessori's description:

We must bear such conditions in mind in order to follow 'progress' in work. The two curves (above and following) represent stages of greatest development. The stage of unrest between the easy and the more difficult work tends to disappear; the child seems more [confident]; and goes more directly and readily to the choice of the culminating exercise.

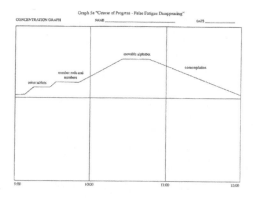

Graph 5a "Course of Progress - False Fatigue Disappearing"

The phase of preparation lasts a very short time, the serious work is of much longer duration; . . . the period of rest, with its characteristic air of comfort and serenity, sets in after the maximum effort has spontaneously spent itself.

Superior stage
Montessori's description:

Even the preparatory work is of a higher kind: as soon as the child comes into the school, [the child] will choose, for instance, the letters of the alphabet, or will write, then (the strenuous work) will read. For recreation, [the child] will choose an intelligent pastime, such as looking at illustrated books. All these intellectual occupations are of a higher order, as are also the moral attributes (obedience, serenity, perseverance). And finally, the work tends to become straight, and parallel to the line of quiescence.

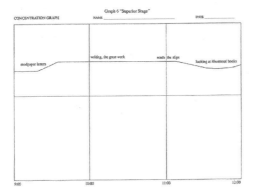

What I always point out is the height of the line as this child enters the class. It is already described as high level of concentration. It might be that this child woke up in the morning excitedly thinking about what was going to be the first work of the day. Or perhaps some large work was allowed to be left out on the table or floor mat at the end of the previous day, and the child can hardly wait to get back to this.

To protect this wonderful beginning of the day it is important to avoid any planned activity, except perhaps a quick handshake or "hello," that would cause the child to forget this purpose, that would prevent the child getting right to work.

The Use of Concentration Graphs

Some teachers, when following the concentration of one child during a three-hour work period, prefer to record the work and the level of concentration in text during the day. Some teachers even look back at the end of the morning and remember what the child did and the depth and length of periods of concentration, and then record it on the prepared graph template.

For myself it worked best (perhaps because I am a visual, right-brained person, and do not think linearly) to record directly onto the prepared graph template. Another reason that I liked working this way was that each time (perhaps every twenty minutes or so) I checked the child I was following, and recorded the work and concentration level, I found myself observing the entire class in the same way. These little pauses throughout the morning were extremely useful as I observed things I wouldn't have seen had I been spending all of my time giving lessons. This meant that the child's concentration graph was complete by the end of the morning so I inserted it directly into the recordkeeping notebook, the section for that child.

Some teachers prefer to do a concentration graph for each child three or more days in a row. This is certainly valid observation, as each child is a little different each day. One has to decide what works best.

In my system of observing one child each day, there was a graph done on each child every six weeks or so, which means several times a year. As soon as I had cycled through all of the children I did a graph for the whole class. It is wonderful, sometimes when one feels like no progress is being made, to go back and look at these graphs to see how the concentration of a child, or the class, has increased over the semester or year.

NOTE: Parent meetings. Rather than focusing first of all on the academic work in class, when I had a meeting with parents, I showed the parents the concentration graphs for their child. This kept the focus on the value of their child learning to independently choose work, to experience deeper and longer periods of concentration, and the positive results of this experience. I found that this was an excellent way for parents not only to begin to understand Montessori, but to look for, and hesitate to interrupt, their child's concentration at home.

Moving Away from Group or Collective Lessons

This presentation is given, not to a group of children, but individually, to help the child to grow mentally. We prepare this special environment to help this growth, to offer freedom so that [the child] can proceed with work in a normal way. The collective lessons are given only to the child who has not yet been normalized. After normalization each child grows individually. One child may be ready for the lesson one day and another child another day . . . If we give a lesson we do not command all the children to stop what they are doing in order to listen. Many children may have absolutely no interest in the lesson and we may bore them.

– Montessori, Creative Development in the Child, The Montessori Approach Vol. II

In using the graph, it is clear that the level of concentration during a group or collective lesson, unless the child has chosen to attend a small group, will be very low. Because this is the motor-sensorial stage of development, where children learn best while moving and not when being required to sit still and listen, the line will often dip below the line of quiescence because a child will often be seen disturbing another out of boredom.

When I have given a workshop on the three-hour work period and the concentration graphs, one of the questions I am always asked is, "When do we do all of the activities that we do in large groups?"

Even the most well-trained Montessori teachers sometimes fall back on teaching in groups even though this was not part of their training. Perhaps it is from memory of one's own education. Or visiting a school and seeing another teacher working this way. So, we talk about how we do everything that is usually done in groups, but in a way more in alignment with Montessori practice.

In the beginning of a new class being established, or in the first days of a new term, or when there is a large group of new children entering an established class, there will be group lessons, even though there will ideally be children already working on their own. But as each child discovered the joy of deep concentration and begins on their own unique path, these larger group activities disappear. Small groups will spontaneously form, a teacher gathering a few newer children, or beginning an activity such as a conversation about the weekend with one child and another joining the conversation, etc. Also, even at this stage of development children sometimes form a group.

I was observing in a class in North Africa and realized that almost all of the children had removed themselves from the classroom and were seated outside as one of their colleagues had gathered them as he led the group in song. He was seated on a chair and the children gathered around him seated on the ground. The teacher and I watched as more children joined in, then then after a few songs they, one by one, left the group and returned to their individual work. The child leader put his chair away and returned to his work.

The following are examples of activities which used to always be taught in groups, and ideas for how to incorporate them into a three-hour work period of uninterrupted concentration.

Reading or telling stories

Curl up in the book corner to read to just one or two children at any time. Or tell a story in the same way. Eventually the children will read and tell stories to each other in the same way.

News time

Impromptu conversations are very important as every child at this age is in the sensitive period for language, speaking, being listened to, then writing and reading. This can begin with one child coming to the teacher wanting to share something exciting that happened at home or on the way to school. Sit down and listen. Another child might join in. Again, the children who are working on their own might be listening and learning about their friends.

Walking on the line

Walking on the line is most successful as an individual activity, not only for developing the physical skill of balance, but mental calmness. It is a perfect example of "teach by teaching rather than correcting" because when a young child tends to run everywhere, instead of being constantly reminded to walk, there are many stages of challenging ways to walk carefully connected with the walking on the line work. The materials for all stages—bell, flag, glass of water, etc. —are available at all times. As with other activities in this list, it is often a small group collective lesson with a group of new students or at the beginning of a new term.

Singing, dancing

When there is no special 'singing time" children are more likely to burst into song when the spirit moves them. Sometimes it is just one child singing from a song card or book or at a table while working. Sometimes a small group forms, with or without the adult.

The directress of a lovely school I once observed in St. John's Wood, London, taught the children to dance in the following way. One child, or a small group, whenever desired, moved a few chairs out of the way, removed their slippers and placed them under a chair, put on a quiet recording of music and danced to the rhythms. Sometimes the directress joined in. The activity was as calm and beautiful as any other in the classroom and the other children continued their own work as the dancing went on.

Playing/working outside

Ideally a Montessori environment is an indoor-outdoor environment for all kinds of activities. In my school in Northern Michigan, where there is deep snow for many months in the winter, we had a large area for dressing and undressing - boots, gloves, snowsuits, etc. The outside area was only available after passing through this dressing room, and it was out of sight of the rest of the classroom for the most part. We had three "outdoor tickets" that children could pin on themselves and go outside whenever they wanted. So even in the most difficult situations outside "play" can be available at any time.

It is important that the outside area be thought out and prepared as carefully as the inside with many important activities such as shoveling snow, pulling weeds, sweeping, and so forth, so that the mind and body can work together on purposeful activities.

Snack

This needs to be thought out according to the culture or country of the school. The steps to preparing-eating-cleaning-up should be analyzed, as in any other practical life activity. The food and manner of eating should be consistent with the country, culture, and tradition. Food should not be taken around and served to other children who are working but should be consumed at the snack table. Then the process, from preparing the snack to cleaning up the snack table, is presented to one child at a time as a lesson.

Other activities

Once we realize the purpose of Montessori is the deep spiritual, mental, and physical healing that occurs through the process of concentration we will apply all of our knowledge, experience, and wisdom to providing this for our children. After applying the above suggestions, it will be very easy to turn all previous "group" activities into individual work. We will all benefit from this effort.

Young people must have enough freedom to allow them to act on individual initiative. But in order that individual action should be free and useful at the same time it must be restricted with certain limits and rules that give the necessary guidance.

— Montessori, *From Childhood to Adolescence*

When through exceptional circumstances work is the result of an inner, instinctive impulse, then even in the adult it assumes a wholly different character. Such work is fascinating, irresistible, and it raises one above deviations and inner conflicts. Such is the work of the inventor or discoverer, the heroic efforts of the explorer, or the compositions of the artist, that is to say, the work of [humans] gifted with such an extraordinary power as to enable them to rediscover the instinct of their species in the patterns of their own individuality. This instinct is then a fountain that bursts through the hard outer crust and rises, through a profound urge, to fall, as refreshing rain, on arid humanity. It is through this urge that the true progress of civilization takes place.

— Montessori, *The Secret of Childhood*

WEEKLY LESSON PLAN

The *weekly lesson plan*, in the form I am going to share with you, is not something I learned in my primary training, but it was developed through my search to find a way to successfully record observations, record details of work, and make plans for future lessons for each child.

Prepared Lesson Plan on the First Day of the Week

Looking through my records of the children's work, I selected several "possible" lessons to give to each child during the week and recorded them on the weekly lesson plan sheet. I kept these plans on two clipboards (two were necessary for a class with 25-30 children) with a pen fastened to it, accessible all day. It was on the top of one of the taller cabinets of materials, out of the sight of the children and easy for me to access at any moment.

In the rectangular box after each child's name, where I had written the suggested lessons, there was room to record suggestions for lessons to be made the following week, corrections to be made, at "a neutral moment," etc. As an example, if I noticed that a child had done the first presentation of the pink tower perfectly and then put it away and moved on to another work in the classroom, I would record "pink tower #2" on the sheet, or even suggest to myself a more detailed challenge of placing the cubes, or to reintroduce the way to carry the cubes to the floor mat in such a way that the differing weights are noticed. Especially with the sensorial work there is the possibility of finer and finer challenges to keep the child focused, to offer opportunities to work toward perfection, and to make the sensorial concepts secure. In my training, we called these little refining movements during a lesson *points of consciousness*. This is because it brings the tiny details and challenges to the consciousness of the child while watching the careful movements of the teacher.

I always wrote the names of the oldest children at the top and the youngest at the bottom. Whenever a moment came, several

44

children wanting/needing a lesson, and I had to choose between the older or the younger in giving lessons, I usually chose the older—because the oldest children are the models for the whole class.

Adrian	clean fish tank division board verb game
Ursula	plant needs exp. skip counting watercolor
Susan	bird-definitions music transposition wash cupboard
Kit	"thank you" geo. cabinet sandpaper letters
John K	close door quietly "I spy" clean carrots
Sarah	walk on line – water poetry cards bathroom

There are three presentations that I planned to give to each child this week. There could be more but keep in mind that the goal is for the child to be able to focus and work on just a few long, involved, challenging "works" in a three-hour work period, rather than a lot of short ones.

ADRIAN: clean fish tank, division board, verb game

URSULA: "plant needs" experiment, skip counting (with long bead chains), water color (advanced)

SUSAN: parts of the bird definition stage, music transposition (with materials), wash cupboard

KIT: "thank you" practice-role playing, geometric cabinet, sandpaper letters

JOHN K.: close door quietly, "I spy" game, clean carrots

SARAH: walk-on-line with glass of water, poetry cards, use the bathroom

The Teacher as Writing Model

The children in the class were very aware of the fact that I was writing notes, with a pencil, on paper throughout the day, so I became an important "writing" model for them. Perhaps this had something to do with the fact that all of these students learned to write around age four, just as we read in Montessori's writings. Children want to learn to do what the adults in their world are doing. They want to read and write if they see us doing these things.

How to Use the Plan During the Day

Whenever I gave a lesson that I had planned for a child I circled it on the worksheet.

When I gave a lesson to the child that was not planned I wrote it in on the worksheet. For example, I might see a child carefully watching a friend doing one of the math activities called the "ten boards" where one combines beads and little number cards to form the numbers 10, 20, 30, 40, and so on, a stage in learning to count from 1 to 99. I am pretty sure that this child is ready for a lesson from me on this material. I would write "ten boards" on the sheet for a lesson in the following week to this child.

When I saw that a child has mastered an activity that was not on the sheet, I wrote it down.

When I saw that a child needed correction that was not an emergency correction that needed to be made immediately, like climbing out the window or cutting off someone's braids, I wrote this down for later. For example, if I notice a child slamming a door I would not correct the child at that moment, but would record "closing door" on the sheet to present later, later in the week or the following week.

Teach by Teaching, Not by Correcting (the Popcorn Game)

How many times might we have said to a child "Say thank you." over the years? When does it ever work? At home, we might record in our minds "practice thank you" rather than reminding or correcting.

In our own family, we created a game to practice just this skill. It was called "the popcorn game." We prepared a large bowl of popcorn. One of us decided to be the host or hostess. That person would offer, "Would you like some popcorn?" The invitee would respond, "Yes, please" and scoop the popcorn out of the bowl into the small bowl and say, "Thank you." The host/hostess would then reply, "You are welcome." The game often would go on and on till the popcorn was gone, turns being taken. Often visiting friends would ask for this game, not just for the popcorn, but because it was so much fun.

Other lessons that might be written down to teach later might be: flush the toilet, wash hands after using the toilet, watching a friend work without interrupting, putting materials away, tuck in chair, and so on.

Adrian	clean fish tank, division board, verb game	Img division observation chair, table of contents
Ursula	plant needs lt, strip counting, water color	short bead frame - mult
Susan	bird - definitions, music - transposition, wash cupboard	bird drawing, flags of world
Kit	"music app", geo. cabinet, sand paper letters	geo. cab cards, shake hands
John K	close door quietly *, "I spy", clean carrots	zip frame *, cut carrots, placing objects
Sarah	walk on line - water, pretty cards, bathroom	walk line - pillow, balloons

Prepared Lesson Plan on the Last Day of the Week

By the end of the week, I have circled those planned presentations that I got to, circled presentations that I made that were not planned ahead, or work mastered that had been presented before.

I have written in lessons or corrections that need to be made the following week

ADRIAN: He had the fish tank and division board lessons, mastered use of a Table of Contents. For the next week, I will write on next week's *weekly lesson plan* for him: verb game (didn't get to it), long division board which I see he is ready for, and present "sitting quietly and observing in the observer's chair" because he is beginning to interrupt another people's work. and something from the *mastery charts.*

URSULA: had "plant needs" experiment and watercolor lesson and mastered the short bead frame - multiplication. Next week I will present skip counting (didn't get to it) and something from the *mastery charts.*

Recording a lesson learned, an activity mastered

If a child mastered an activity, I recorded on the weekly lesson plan sheet, and placed an asterix (*) next to that activity to alert myself that this work was done correctly, that the child clearly understood the steps.

Last day of the week, preparation for the following week

At the end of each week I recorded the information from the weekly lesson plan on the *mastery charts* (covered in the following chapters). Then it was clear what lessons each child had been given, which they had mastered, and what lessons, or further challenges, they were ready for next. From this information, I could prepare the weekly lesson plan for the next week.

A schedule

For myself Monday was the first day of the lesson plan use, and Friday the last day, the day for planning the following week. But the plan depends on the teacher's schedule. For some I have found that it was best to start the plan on another day because there was no time to work on recordkeeping, and create the next weekly lesson plan on Friday.

MASTERY CHARTS INTRODUCTION

There are many systems for keeping track of presentation and mastery of the lessons over the years in the primary class. As a teacher makes the weekly lesson plan it is necessary to know just what activities each child has had a lesson on and which ones have then been mastered.

I made a graph, *a mastery chart,* for each of the areas in the classroom. The following is an example of part of the graph for the area first presented to a new child. It is called "Steps to Freedom" or "Preliminary Exercises." Later in this chapter there is more information on this and the other areas.

Recording a Presentation/Lesson

During class, weekly lesson plan

After giving a 1:1 presentation or lesson that I had written on the *weekly lesson plan* page (explained in the last chapter) I drew a circle around that lesson to show that the lesson had indeed been given.

If I observed that the child had been given a 1:1 lesson by another child, or had begun to work on it after carefully watching another child, I also recorded is on the weekly lesson plan, also with a circle around it to show the lesson had been given.

Let us say that a child had had a lesson on the zipper dressing frame, that gives practice in preparing to zip one's clothing. I would record "zipper" on the weekly lesson plan, and then circle it.

After class or at the end of the week, mastery chart

Later, to show that the child had been given that zipper lesson, I would draw a diagonal line in the square for "zipper" after the child's name.

Recording the Mastery of an Activity

During class, weekly lesson plan:

If I observed that a child has mastered an activity that was not on the weekly lesson plan, I recorded, circled it, and added an asterix (*) to show it has been mastered.

After class or at the end of the week, mastery chart:

Later, to show that the child had mastered an activity, I crossed the original diagonal mark, making an "X."

Write in front of the children!

As I have said before, I believe it is very helpful for the children to see the teacher writing with a pen or pencil regularly. Today I know that there are teachers who have begun to record their lessons and lesson planning on a computer screen, during class, and in front of the children.

This is not a good idea for two reasons:

1 – Screens.

We adults are the models for the children. If they see us working on computer screens during class that will reinforce what they are seeing outside the classroom, that screens are the preferred way to work. We are actually "teaching" children to depend on screens which is antithetical to the work of many wise educators, which is to keep screens out of the environment, school, or home, as long as possible,

2 – *Beautiful Handwriting.* We go to great length in the primary class to indirectly (large muscle work) and directly (rough and smooth boards, knobs, sandpaper letters) prepare children not only to write, but to write beautifully, in a way they will be proud of. However, we all know that children at this age want to do what their adults (at home and school) are doing. So, it is very good when they see the teacher (and the parent) happily writing on paper with a pencil or pen. Even better if their adults are modeling lovely handwriting.

There will come a time later for learning keyboard skills and valuable use of computer screens, but research shows that there are many valuable neurological, social, and self-image reasons for children to learn to write beautifully on paper.

Creating Mastery Charts

The creation of mastery charts is personal because it is important that it makes sense and is enjoyable. If this is not the case the teacher will not look forward to this work. I wanted to cover each area on one squared piece of paper, so I could easily note the lessons of the class as a whole. As you read further in this book, you will see suggested lists of activities in each area.

In my primary classes, when creating the mastery charts for the beginning of each year, I chose 25-30 of the most important activities from each area. These lists in no way encompass all of the materials and presentations possible. However, it does keep the class balanced, and each child's exposure to the amazing variety of lessons in the Montessori classroom rich and full.

A teacher will continue to refer to the training course albums, and to add lessons to the plan, growing along with the children.

Seeing All of the Mastery Charts and the Progress of All Child at Once

I found it essential in my work to be able to visually scan the work of the whole class, in all areas, at one time.

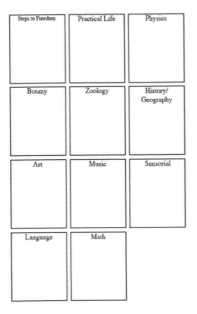

Consulting with a teacher in the Bahamas years ago, I suggested that she take the mastery charts for all of the areas out of her notebook and put them all together on the wall back in her apartment, as there was no office or teachers' room at the school. She was a bit grumbly because there was so much else to do, but she humored me and did it that night.

The next day she came running, smiling, into the classroom, delighted with what she had seen. "You are so right how important it is to see everything at once!" were her words. Now she could understand that there were areas in the classroom that she was practically ignoring. She could see that the happiest students, those who were concentrating deeply on work, were those who had mastered many more lessons than the others. She saw that a new little girl who just had not settled down, had received very few lessons, so no wonder she was having trouble!

When it is necessary for a person to leaf through an album (or scroll through the same thing on a computer) to check on children's lessons, or the teacher's lessons in different areas, it is not possible to see the whole picture.

With the charts for each of the seven areas of learning hung on the wall, all visible at one time, it was easy to tell, in an instant, what areas or lessons are ahead and behind, and which children might be receiving a lot of lessons, or lessons in just a few areas. Then I could see instantly how to plan the next step for each academic area, and each child.

Practical Points

Size of Mastery Charts:

As you can see in the "steps to freedom" chart earlier in this chapter, I put the first name of each child on the left side of each chart, and I chose 25-35 lessons in each area for the top. I made my own charts with 1/3" squares, making the chart size about 15" x 15". That way I had plenty of room for all of the six charts all placed next to each other on the wall of the office.

Where to Keep Mastery Charts:

My first year I taped the charts to the inside of two high cupboard doors that were in my classroom. That year I hadn't yet developed the *weekly lesson plan* system, so I needed to have access to these charts all during the day. From the second year on, thanks to the *weekly lesson plan* system, I kept the charts in my office-storage room.

It is best to keep mastery charts out of sight of visitors. During my parent conferences, they were not visible, nor were they referred to.

Color:

I chose a color for each year. If I carried forward a chart from one year to the next, I used a different color so I could keep track of the presentations by year. When I redid the graphs to prepare for the beginning of each new year, copying from the last chart, I kept to this color system.

Annual Re-Creation of Mastery Charts:

In the primary class of my own school, it was possible for children to enter the day after their second birthday and many stayed through kindergarten and occasionally first grade, from age two to seven. As a result, some of the children were there for five years. With space only for thirty children I only had room for a few new children each year. So, the new, very young, students were placed at the bottom of each chart. Ours was a stable community in a small town so children were almost never removed from the school. For these reasons, I didn't have to redo my *mastery charts* every year. However, I enjoyed redoing them, seeing the amazing work that had been done; this was a celebration when preparing for a new year.

MASTERY CHART, STEPS TO FREEDOM
First Lessons for a New Child

The first lessons and materials a child is offered when first joining the class, first entering the classroom, are called "steps to freedom" activities, or "preliminary exercises." These activities give a child a feeling of security in this new environment. They help the child learn to function independently, to be relaxed and happy in the classroom, to be able to arrive each day and start working.

To decide what activities to include in your own environment, put yourself in the place of a new child entering the school for the first time. What objects in this environment first meet the eye? Then think of what basic activities are necessary for a child to feel comfortable. Although there will be small group activities, such as singing and practical life games if there are several new children entering at once, as a rule the lessons on how to carry, use, and put away these first toys, are taught by the teacher to each child. If the child makes a mistake we do not correct, but repeat the next day.

Below is a suggested list of "steps to freedom" toys that might be found in a Western Montessori primary class. The selection and placing of a table mat or floor mat define one's work space and is especially helpful because it is the first task carried out when a child begins to work, and it is a way of marking a work space as the child goes to a shelf to pick up the chosen materials.

Along with defining the child's work space or the following activity, selecting and placing one's table or floor mat marks the beginning of a work cycle. And replacing it at the end of the activity marks the end of a work cycle. This is a very important first step in learning to be able to function happily in the class.

Opening and closing the classroom door

Putting on, and taking off, shoes and *inside* slippers, coat, mittens, etc.

Hanging up a coat

Putting *inside* slippers (if used) in the bag at the end of the day

Greeting the teacher by shaking hands

Using the toilet

Washing hands

Getting a drink of water

Taking a table/work mat from a shelf and placing it on a table

Selecting a floor mat and placing it on the floor

Selecting a link-with-the-home toy and taking it to the table/floor mat

Sitting on a chair

Returning a *toy* to the correct shelf

Folding/rolling table mat and returning it to the shelf

Placing a chair under the table when finished working

Carrying and unrolling a floor mat

Rolling and returning a floor mat to its place

Placing objects quietly on a table or shelf

Walking around floor mats

Opening and closing containers

Link-with-the-home Toys

The first materials that a new child will be invited to select from a shelf are not the official Montessori didactic materials. This is because the focus of the learning is picking up an item, carrying it to the table or floor mat, exploring it, and then returning it to its place on the shelf. Mastering this process is very satisfying to a new child.

These materials, or toys, are kept near the entrance to the classroom so they will be the first items encountered by a child just joining the class.

In some places children do not have toys but instead spend their time collaborating with the other members of the family, on the daily work of the family. This is a very healthy situation but it demands a little creativity in selection of the very first activities. One year I was helping to set up the very first Montessori class in Paro, Bhutan, and monitoring the new teacher over the first days. As there are no toys as a rule in homes in this country, we created sorting exercises with familiar little bowls and objects such as seeds and buttons, and beads to string. We also put out a few knobbed puzzles that had been donated to the school but not used. This served very well, allowing the children to practice this new role in the function of the class. I observed several children watching other children going through this cycle and I could just imagine their satisfaction in figuring out the process.

We were able, very quickly, to move on to dressing frames, drawing, sweeping with small versions of typical Bhutanese brooms that we had made, setting out the lunches that were brought from home—beginning the practical life work.

Removing These Toys

Link-with-the-home toys are removed as soon as the child starts to concentrate on the other activities which require more logical steps of purposeful activity, more logical thinking, and longer periods of concentration.

When the first *casa dei bambini* environment in Rome was initially created, Montessori included dolls and other fantasy toys in the environment. She discovered, however, that once the children were given the means to do real work in the environment, work that they had seen being carried out in the home since birth, the attraction to make-believe and traditional toys disappeared. This same transition is observed all over the world today.

Even though these toys are removed a few weeks into a new semester, if a child begins in the class in the middle of the year some of these toys will be brought back into the classroom for that child.

Here is a list of *link-with-the-home* materials/toys that might be found in a Western Montessori primary class:

Knobbed puzzles

Sorting trays, with small bowls and familiar items to sort

Metal nuts and bolts

Mosaic blocks

Bead stringing, several sizes

Small set of blocks

Crayons and paper

Individual blackboard and chalk

MASTERY CHART, PRACTICAL LIFE

The emphasis here should not be on the word *practical*, but on the word *life*. This work provides a link with the home when a child is just entering the school. It is reassuring to see all of the objects and the activities, at school, that have been observed at home. They are an aid to life because they help the children to adapt to their time and place in history and in the world. There are no "Montessori" practical life activities, but only those that exist in the child's environment. They depend on the culture of the child.

Some parents may object to these activities and want the child to get down to the business of learning to read and write. But before these subjects can be approached there are many other needs of the child that must be met, and abilities which must be acquired. These needs are first met by the practical life activities. In fact, there are no other activities that can assist the total development, mental, physical, and spiritual, as do these activities.

Their aim is to help children to do, in a more perfect and orderly and satisfying manner, those things that they already want to do according to their own natural impulses. Children want to explore and imitate, and to master according to their stage of development, all of those activities that have been going on around them since birth.

A First-Year Example

A friend of mine who had no funds to purchase Montessori materials for her first year of teaching told me later that she had had only practical life and language materials, easily gathered, and created by her and the parents of the new school. She said that it was a wonderful year, one of her best ever. She and the parents focused on analyzing the practical life of the daily home life, and that of the local culture, in creating activities, and the language work focused on oral language and preparation for later writing and reading.

A Discovery by Montessori

In the very first class, in Rome, Dr. Montessori one day noticed that a child's nose was running and needed to be cleaned. Rather than cleaning it herself, she showed a child how to blow one's nose, and then clean it, correctly. After this first lesson on taking care of one's own needs, it was the children who asked for more such. It was the children who wanted to do the things that were being done by an adult. The practical life lessons helped Montessori make one of the most important discoveries in the potential of young children which was the natural need or tendency to be independent, and to do real work.

Practical Life Work is Cultural

At the Maria Montessori Institute in London where I took my first training course in 1970-1971 there were students from all over the world. One day we were asked to share the way we had been taught to greet another person. One student demonstrated the correct way for a girl to curtsy, another placed her hands together as if in prayer to honor the other, and some showed the correct way to shake hands or kiss a cheek.

As a result of this demonstration we understood the reason why, in creating practical life activities for classrooms, we must focus on observing our own culture when we returned home. The practical life activities appropriate for children growing up in England would not be the same for a child living in Norway or Senegal. Also, many schools are multi-cultural so practical life should reflect the home life of all of the students.

We were taught, in fine detail, how to analyze the details of an activity, and then to read out steps we had written down to another adult to see if our analysis of the steps was correct, confusing, or incomplete, or clear and complete. I have used this method to help people all over the world understand how to teach children practical life.

61

Direct and Indirect Aims of Practical life

Each practical life activity has a clearly observed *direct aim* such as improving eye-hand control or independence, or learning how to set a table or tie one's shoes. But often there are also one or more *indirect aims* which prepare the child for future accomplishments.

For example, if one were to offer a lesson on washing a table, with no early preparation, it could not be successful because there are so many steps. There is clearly a need to master skills with the indirect aim of preparing a child for such a long and involved task. Such activities as putting on an apron, carrying a pitcher of water without spilling, pouring liquid, cleaning up water spilled on the floor, carrying out steps of an activity in logical order, replacing used cloths with fresh ones, and so on—all of these, when mastered, contain the indirect aim of preparing a child to be able to succeed at washing a table. This is true for most, if not all, of the practical life work

Three Areas of Practical Life

At this level, there are three areas of practical life:

Caring for oneself

Caring for the environment

Grace and courtesy

It is very important to keep in mind that these activities are real and important and necessary. For example, in the use of clothes pins—these should not be used as busywork, meaningless attaching of clothes pins to the edge of a tin can (which sadly I have seen in classrooms when consulting.) They should be used to fasten cloth, such as metal polishing cloths that have been washed in another classroom practical life activity, to a line to dry. Later, when dry, these same cloths might be put in a basket next to an ironing board with a real, child-safe iron, to be later ironed, folded, and put away by another child.

Rotation of Materials

There are several areas of the class where materials are rotated. For example, the physics activities, contents of sets of vocabulary cards, and the art on the walls. In practical life, there may be changes to make the room more interesting, new flower vases, aprons, and so on; but the basic materials for caring for the environment and oneself should be permanent. Just as in the home, a child should be able to find the broom and dustpan always ready, the materials for washing a table, the tissue paper and mirror to clean one's nose, and so on. This is the children's house and they take pride, and learn a lot, in caring for it, just as they do learning to take care of themselves.

Although there are many more practical life activities than those I have listed for this basic practical life mastery chart, these are the ones I always included in a class in the United States.

Practical Life: Caring for Oneself

Use of an umbrella

Blowing one's nose

Washing hands

Cleaning the sink

Cleaning nails

Dressing frames: button, snap, buckle, zip, lace, tie, snap, etc.

Using an apron

Setting a table

Combing or brushing hair

Brushing teeth

Feeding oneself, use of utensils

Cleaning or polishing shoes

Practical Life: Caring for the Environment

Fastening an apron

Moving and placing a table or chair silently

Placing objects on a table or shelf carefully and silently

Putting away work, replacing what might need to be replaced, cotton balls for example

Dusting

Cleaning up spills

Mopping

Folding

Sweeping

Polishing mirrors and windows

Polishing metal objects

Setting and clearing a table

Washing dishes

Washing a shelf

Washing a table

Washing a chair

Washing cloths

Hanging up cloths to dry with clothes pins

Ironing

Practical Life: Grace and Courtesy

Manners are very specific to a culture, and will include activities that the children will have seen outside the classroom. In the classroom, they are taught first by means of the adult in the environment as a model, and then by means of enjoyable games, one child at a time or a small group of children who might be between periods of their own individual work,

These are examples of what one might find in a Western Montessori classroom:

Greeting another person

Saying "please" and "thank you"

Offering something to another

Helping another child with an apron, a coat, etc.

Placing objects gracefully

Carrying items without dropping or spilling

Serving food

Table manners

Sitting or rising gracefully and quietly

Speaking in a normal voice

Looking at someone when speaking to them

Looking to see if someone is busy so as not to interrupt

Carrying scissors

Handing scissors to another person

Walking on the Line and the Silence Game

These activities are important elements of practical life, grace, and courtesy. They deserve their own place in this chapter.

Walking on the Line

The equilibrium of the body is the key to perfecting many varied movements. Walking on the Line is a method for helping little children to possess this equilibrium, to keep their balance safely, and at the same time, to perfect the most essential movement, walking.

There should ideally be a permanent ellipse in the classroom. It can be made with tape very easily, and I have even seen it made with tile inlaid in the classroom floor. I always recommend that something, a bookcase or table and chair, be kept in the middle of this large ellipse, so there will be no temptation to have children sit on the line for collective lessons.

First a child learns to walk freely, placing the foot completely on the line so that the line lies along the axis of the flat part of the foot. The toe and heel must both be on the line. While focusing on these aspects an effort is necessary to maintain equilibrium. When a child can do this well, we give another difficulty to overcome, walking on the line so that the heel of the foot in front is touching the toe of the foot in back, walking heel to toe. Then various other stages or challenges are offered—carrying a flag on the open palm of one's hand, later with a flag in each hand, walking with a lit candle so slowly that it is not extinguished, walking with a pillow on one's head that doesn't fall off, carrying a soup bowl of water (especially valuable in a class where children will be carrying bowls of hot soup at lunch), and many others—are presented as the usual 1:1 lessons, the teacher showing one child. It is quite common for children to come up with their own challenges at this point.

Sometimes, in the beginning of a new class for example, or at the beginning of a new term with several new children, it is presented to a group of children. But most of the time walking on the line is an individual activity carried out at any time during the day.

Walking on the line is always a choice, and I have seen children choose this activity as they feel the need, not only to carefully challenge themselves physically, but as an opportunity to process and to think!

There can be music playing quietly in the background, controlled by the children, but this is not to get the children to move to the musical rhythms; it is meant as a pleasant background. Moving to music and various rhythms is another activity altogether and is carried out independently of this line. As far as making your practical life mastery chart you can decide how many walking on the line stages to include. Here are some suggestions:

Walking on the line

Toe-heel walking on the line

Walking on the line with a glass of water

Walking on the line carrying a flag

Walking on the line carrying a lit candle

Walking on the line carrying a basket on head

Joining another who is walking on the line

The Silence Game

The *silence game* is not for imposing silence on a noisy class. It is an inhibition of movement which requires an effort and comes from the will. It is a magical activity that is introduced with a story, then begun by the teacher or played after silence arises spontaneously, and always ends with the teacher whispering the name of each child, calling him to join her silently. It is really wonderful when used correctly.

There is much indirect preparation to be done before expecting the whole of the *silence game* to be successful. We break down the exercise and introduce various parts ahead of time. First the children must be ready to cooperate with you. They must trust you and you must trust them. They must know how to listen. They must know how to sit still in their chairs or on the floor.

You can make a game of this, sit still in a chair without moving until approached and asked, "What are you doing?" and you can explain, "I am sitting still." Almost always the child will want to try this. (This is "sitting still" not "making silence") You can invite this child(ren) to close their eyes and listen to the sounds. When all of the children can do this you can explain, "When everyone is sitting still and making no noise, we call that 'silence'".

Next prepare a pretty plaque with the word silence on it on one side and a pretty picture on the other and hang it in the classroom with the picture showing. One day when you are talking about silence, show the plaque and the word.

In order to play the silence game, you must judge your time so you can finish the game. One day turn around the sign so silence is showing, Sit perfectly still in a chair. The class will become still. Do this long enough so the class can appreciate the silence, but not so long that they become bored.

Be sure you have a list of all of the children present on that day so no one will be left out of the game. Walk noiselessly out of the room or sit where you are hidden behind a curtain or bookcase in the classroom. Very quietly and slowly, almost whispering, call each child to join you. When all of the children have joined you, the game is over and slowly and quietly, you as model, everyone returns to their work.

I have a lovely memory of an occurrence during the first year of opening my own school, the first Montessori school in the whole of Northern Michigan. We had begun in a traditional Catholic school, being given a room on the second floor of a wing of the school that was not being used. According to the floor space requirement we were only allowed 19 children, so my assistant had her own material-making table and very little interaction with the children.

The head of the department of social services for Northern Michigan had arranged to come a long distance to observe as she had never seen a Montessori class before and was very suspicious, having heard the typical complaint—too rigid, too free, etc.

As she sat and watched the children, they all became so busy and focused that the room became completely quiet. As I sometimes did at these moments, I hung up our little "silence" sign and gradually some of the children noticed, and smiled, as they knew what was coming.

Very quietly I picked up my list of children, double checked to see that they were all present on that day, and walked across the room and sat on the floor in the book corner, invisible to most of the children. They waited expectantly. Very quietly I whispered the name of the first child, who then quietly stood up, tucked the chair underneath her table, and very quietly tip-toed across the room, sitting silently next to me. One by one I whispered the name of each child and each one joined me in, and next to, the small book corner. When we were all seated we stayed there for about a minute, savoring the silence "that we had created together." And they quietly returned to their work.

The observer was astounded. She became sold on the potential of Montessori, and from then on came for an annual observation and meal together, and she sent many people to observe our class over the years.

As far as making your silence game section of the practical mastery chart/charts you can decide how many lines to have. Here are some suggestions:

Silence game introduction (I followed, each year, the example of Montessori and brought a sleeping baby into the class to show the children how skilled even an infant can be holding still and being quiet).

Other steps in preparing for the game

Silence game sign

Silence game calling out names

After such exercises, it seemed to me that their love for me was greater: they certainly became more obedient, sweeter, and gentler. We had passed a few moments of intimacy among ourselves . . .
— Montessori, *The Discovery of the Child*

Practical Life of the Culture Subjects

The culture areas described in the next chapter—physics, botany, zoology, geography, history, art, and music—are the basis of the classroom. Each area has specific practical life. Examples in the art area would include washing a table, water jar, mixing dish; washing an easel and plastic floor mat (I have often seen a child paint a picture just to get to the work of cleaning the easel and floor mat, obviously enjoying the cleaning up as much as painting!), washing brushes, sharpening pencils, washing blackboard, sweeping up after paper cutting.

MASTERY CHARTS,
THE CULTURE SUBJECTS

The culture area is essential as our goal is to help children adapt and thrive at their particular time and place on earth, and begin the preparation for being a compassionate member of the human family. One of the most enjoyable elements in being a Montessori teacher is that we keep learning, in all areas of life, right along with our students. Over the years I have come to understand that, after practical life, the culture subjects—physics, botany, zoology, history, geography, music, and art—should be considered when preparing the environment for children at this age.

The practical life work in the primary class gives tools and skills for caring for the environment. The sensorial work opens eyes to explore the environment with all of the senses. The language work gives the tools for speaking, writing, and reading about the world, and the math introduces the tools for measuring and comparing the elements of the world. And all of this work is richer with the culture areas as their basis.

This is the age of the absorbent mind, when all impressions are taken in effortlessly and completely, becoming part of one. The elements of culture that are experienced at this age provide a special sensitivity later in life. Something as simple as learning to wash the leaves of a plant is a first step to caring about plants throughout life. Being casually aware of small representations of great art hanging at the child's eye level can be the beginning of an interest in art. Learning that the elements of an electric circuit—light bulb, battery, connecting wires—must be complete in order for the light to turn on, can awaken a lifelong interest in the laws of physics.

Here are the details of providing this broad cultural basis.

1 – The rich and complete classroom culture. At this age, rather than taking children out on field trips, we give "keys" to all of the

cultural elements in the classroom. In this way, all areas of the world can be explored first in the class, then in the home and neighborhood. I always had a small area of the classroom for each of the cultural areas, and I kept the language materials for each in that area. Books related to each area can also be kept in these areas rather than in the book corner.

2 – Each cultural area in the class has specific practical life activities that are related.

3 – The sensorial keys—size, weight, color, smell, temperature, taste, texture, and so on—inspire children to explore these areas in finer than normal detail. Assembling the electric circuit and working with continent puzzle maps, for example, are sensorial keys specific to the physics and geography areas.

4 – The correct and exact language, "Norway maple" rather than "tree", or "Russian Blue cat" rather than "kitty" prepare children to express themselves clearly and specifically, first with spoken and sung language and later in writing.

5 – Last of all we provide handwork and further activities in each area, to explore and express, and become aware of this new knowledge as it grows and changes. It also is the beginning of the discovery of how different areas of knowledge are connected. Examples might be combining the world of plants and the world of art by making prints with potatoes or leaves. Or singing combining language and geography by learning songs of a variety of languages, and from different countries.

Teaching the Teacher

It is not enough for the teacher to love the child. She must first love and understand the universe. She must prepare herself, and truly work at it.
— Montessori, *From Childhood to Adolescence*

In the first weeks of my first Montessori teacher training course we combined the learning of Montessori philosophy with actual explorations in London. We visited museums and collected art postcards, and found examples of different leaf shapes and leaf attachments to a stem, which provided a hands-on experience, and a growing interest, in botany that was covered in detailed in the course. We pulled together this research in a teacher's album called the General Knowledge album. This album was intended to be added to over the years.

During the first AMI 3-6 class in Morocco, directed by my good friend Lhamo Pemba, I gave the lectures in the culture areas. These lectures included how to create the teacher's general knowledge album, the teacher's own personal leaf collection, and the beginning of a language album, sometimes called *formal language* or *poetry and song* album. Over the years I added to the language album more than any other as I discovered which nursery rhymes, poems, and songs were most loved by the children.

All of these lectures have been pulled together, along with the culture lectures for creating these areas of the classroom, in the book *The Red Corolla, Montessori Cosmic Education for 3-6.*

Creating the Culture Mastery Charts

It is up to you to create the list for each area, including the practical life, sensorial, language, and other lessons. The point is to have a balance, so one area is not covered less or more than the others. For language, each area has specific language materials including classified picture and reading cards, "parts of" cards, and definition reading stages.

Here are some examples of what might be listed in each area, in each mastery chart. I am taking these examples directly from complete lists in the *Red Corolla* book:

Physics

Only a few of these examples would be on the physics shelf at one time, and you might not present all of them in one term, so you would need to take this into consideration for your mastery chart.

Simple circuit

Shadows

Magnet sorting

Sand and iron filings

Compass

Blowing bubbles

Candle in limited air

Bicycle pump

Syphoning

Funnel

Vacuum

Rising hot air

The arch

Camera

Sound

Sink and float

Pendulum

Prism

Botany

Care of plants, inside and outside of the class, is basic to this area. Exploring comes first and then language. I have seen many environments where the language materials that follow this exploration and experience is very limited, often only parts of plant, flower, leaf, and then the nature cabinet. But there is so much more for the teacher to learn about, and then to share with the children.

On my mastery chart for this area I kept track of the plant experiments, then the language and language material, classified cards (examples are classifying plants into herbs, garden flowers, fruit, vegetables, etc.), and then parts of, and definitions. Today this work is especially important because children who have deep and broad botany experiences are far more likely to care about the environment of the planet as adults.

Outside - raking leaves

Inside - dusting and washing leaves

Watering plants

Flower arranging

Nature table

Leaf cabinet

Leaf cabinet cards

Needs of plant experiments (there are four)

Gravitropism

Phototropism

Exploration and then language cards:

Parts of plant, flower, leaf, root, bulb, etc.

Leaves: venation, margins, attachment, etc.

Flowers: types of corollas, pistils, etc.

Types of roots and their parts

Types of fruit and their parts

Zoology

Just as with the botany work, we give experiences both inside the classroom and outside. For inside, it is important to think of animals as temporary guests, and to put their needs above our learning about them. The first lessons are how to touch, hold, and feed animals. Containers must be clean and comfortable and ideally, temporary. Insects and other invertebrates can be brought in for one day, or even found in the classroom. These can include worms, centipedes, ants, ladybugs and so on.

Since we try to give children experience with all of the vertebrates, fish can be kept in a classroom aquarium, amphibians and reptiles and mammals can be visitors, and birds are best experienced by the use of outside birdfeeders rather than cages. For example, watching what kinds of birds are attracted to birdfeeders, and being able to see close up the variety of types of birds and the parts of beaks, tails, etc.

Just as in the botany area, children who have early experiences caring for animals, learning to understand their needs and to appreciate the variety, might well want to learn about and protect the diversity of life on earth later.

For my mastery chart record for this area I keep track of what animals I had arranged to bring into the classroom for the children to experience, and then the language material, classified cards sets of various aspects of plants, reading and definition stages. Here are some examples:

Invertebrates

Fish

Amphibians

Reptiles

Birds

Mammals

Domestic animals

Wild animals

Farm animals

Pets

Kinds of cats

Then the reading and definition card material for the five classes of vertebrates, and the external parts of their bodies. (Internal parts study is for the 6-12 class for several reasons.)

Geography and History

In my classes, these were together on the shelves. Most classes have the Montessori globes, land forms, and puzzle maps. Land and water forms—cape, bay, island, lake, etc. —ideally are formed by the children with clay. I found this much more a learning experience than using pre-made forms that require no more work than adding water. These are the beginning explorations of the physical planet. The language materials give practice in talking about them, and will encourage more detailed exploration of maps and globes.

Peoples of the world materials teach that the physical needs of humans throughout history have depended on the environment. For example, there are very real physical reasons why the clothing and houses and foods in a tropical environment are different in different parts of the world, for example where there is snow year around, or where a culture has developed in the mountains, or rain forest. This is a logical introduction to the cultural differences of the peoples of the world.

Continent folders, if included in your class, should be sure to include both the ancient and modern aspects of each continent. And the pictures should represent only the physical needs of humans: food, transportation, clothing, and housing. These are aspects of life that children can see and touch in their daily life. The mental and spiritual needs of humans are the study of the child in the 7-12 class, where the exploration is more by the imagination than by the senses.

Language and handwork

There is detailed language material, including definitions, of the land and water forms. Also, card materials classifying the physical needs of clothing, houses, transportation, food, to be kept in this area of the classroom. Handwork gives further understanding of these areas. Books for these subjects can be kept in this area or in the library or book corner.

The events chart and the child's personal timeline are the two main works of the child in the history area at this age. Here are suggestions for your mastery charts for this area:

Globe showing land and water

Land and water forms (island, lake, cape, bay, gulf, peninsula, isthmus, strait)

Classified land and water cards

Definitions

Globe showing continents in color

Puzzle map of the world

Puzzle map of the continent of the school

Puzzle map of the country of the school

Puzzle map of other continents

Map with flags

Peoples of the world

Events chart

Personal timeline

Music

Just as with language, the specific elements of music are explored before a child is ready to work with the Montessori bells. In preparing the environment there will be CDs of music and a way for an individual child to choose and listen to this music quietly but NOT with earphones (for several reasons). There can be books about music as played in different cultures, and showing classical and ethnic musical instruments, and composers, kept ideally in the music area. Also picture cards for songs.

Singing is not listed here but it occurs daily. The growing collection of the teacher's poetry/song album is the basis. Here is an example of how I shared these with the children.

For my classes I made a card for each song (just as for each poem and nursery rhyme) with a small picture at the top. These were kept in the music area of the class. A child would go to the box and leaf through the cards that were standing upright in the box. It was easy to identify which card the child wanted because the picture at the top was related to the song. Sometimes the child would bring the card to me or to an older child to sing together. Sometimes the child, even though unable to read yet, would stand there and sing the song. Sometimes a couple of children would pick out a card and sing together. And at times, the other children in the class, even though busy at their own work, would join in and sing.

As a musician, I was especially interested in learning more in this area from the well-known Montessorian Sanford Jones. So, I have included his recommendations in my work, at both the primary and elementary levels. Here are the activities I included on my mastery chart for music:

Rhythm – heartbeat

Rhythm – matching a pulse

Rhythm – children's names

Rhythm – stepping

Rhythm – conducting forms

Musical pitches – with the body

Musical pitches – finishing a phrase

Timbre – percussion instruments

Timbre – human voice

Timbre – the environment

Piano and forte

Tempo

Moving to music/dancing

In-house concerts

Recording – ethnic music

Recordings – composers

Recordings – instruments

The following is not in the *Red Corolla* book but this work is always included in the teacher's albums of any AMI 3-6 course. I have found that not many teachers get through this work because there is an unwarranted feeling that one needs to be a trained musician to do so. In fact, the Montessori bells are just like any other sensorial materials. During training the adults spend many hours learning this work through presenting them to other adults, until they can master the work and the presentation of the work. And then it is easy to present them to children. Here is a list of what would be included in the music mastery chart for this work:

Pairing/matching bells

Grading the bells

Naming the bells

Notation board #1

Notation board #1 and #2

Composition

Sight reading boards

Intervals

Black bells

Diatonic scale

Pentatonic scale

Chromatic scale

Sharps and flats

Treble and bass clef

Chords

Tone bars

Art

An attractive, colorful, clean environment, with small framed pictures—reflecting all of the culture areas—hung at the child's eye level, is a good start for awakening a sensitivity for art in children. Just like the practical life materials, the collection of art materials stays the same. The practical life materials are there to allow caring for the environment, by the adult or children, at any time. The art materials are there so that whenever a child is inspired to express something being learned or felt, the means to do so are available. The teacher's supply of extra art materials should be out of sight of the children. This will help to keep the environment beautiful and not a visual distraction.

Books on schools of art, or cultural art, children's biographies of artists, even art methods, can be kept here or in the book corner or library. Also, there can be classified card materials (such as sculpture, architecture, oil paintings, mobiles, etc.), art of the child's country, art of other traditions, famous paintings containing animals, well-known artists. Here is a list of suggested materials to be shown to each child and listed on the mastery chart:

Crayons

Pencils

Easel painting

Watercolor

Clay - coil

Clay - slab

Clay – pinch

Print making

Paper cutting – strips

Cutting – single folds

Cutting – circles

Collage

Cards – schools of art

Cards – kinds of art

Cards – artists

Classroom library: each cultural area should have a good supply of books to reinforce what the children are learning. If there are a few favorites, keep them out all the time, but remove them when no one looks at them for a while. Also have a wonderful library in storage for constant rotation.

MASTERY CHART,
THE SENSORIAL WORK

*We call it material for the development of the senses,
but sense development is merely the consequence of the
urge to do something with the hands. The children also
gain the ability to control their movements with precision,
and this skill brings them closer to maturity.*
— Montessori, *The 1946 London Lectures*

The senses educated and refined by use of the sensorial materials are: visual (eyes), aural or auditory (ears), gustatory (taste), tactile (touch), baric (weight), thermic (temperature), olfactory (nose), and stereognostic (touching and moving, or the tactile and muscular sense together.) An example of stereognostic work is when a child, who has been through the early steps of working with the sensorial materials, then works with the material while blindfolded.

The sensorial materials, when used correctly, give the child an understanding of such qualities as size, length, width, color, taste, weight, texture, shape, and sound—helping to make sense of the thousands of impressions in the environment, and eventually to express them through language.

These materials have a built-in *control of error* so a child can do the work at any time, and repeat it as often as necessary, working toward perfection, without the permission or help of the adult. When the work has been perfected, and the concept abstracted, the child will finish with this material and will move on to something else. The child decides when this is, not the adult.

Over the many years of Montessori work, there are a few points that I have found myself making over and over:

1. The sensorial materials taught in a Montessori teacher training course have been tested and refined for over one hundred years all over the world which is why they work.

2. Each piece of material, and each lesson on the correct way to use it, is a unique "key" that encourages children to explore the world in finer and finer detail.

3. Only one key is necessary to open a door, so duplications confuse the children.

Use and Mis-Use of Materials

As with all of the Montessori materials, it has become very clear over the years that when these materials are used the way they are taught in Montessori teacher training, everything falls into place and we have the desired results in the development of children. But when a piece of material, a unique key to the world, is used for another purpose—combining several sets of materials in building a castle for example—it stops being a key and creates confusion.

Using the pink tower as an example, a child first receives the two main presentations of the pink tower (on the same day or different days depending on the child) placing the blocks one on top of the other concentrically, and doing the same but with one corner of each cube coinciding. Following the mastery of these two ways of building the tower there can be a further challenge in handling the materials, or building the tower from a distance, or an extension of exploring the room with the new concepts of large and small. These extensions give practice in thinking and understanding the concept more deeply. The accompanying language makes these concepts part of the child's working vocabulary: *small, large, smaller, larger, smallest, largest.* Later a child might be shown how to assemble the tower blindfolded, now becoming a stereognostic exercise.

These are the steps of the correct use of this piece of material.

There is certainly value in children exploring with the sensorial materials, for example comparing the brown/broad stair with the pink tower by lining them up together. But we are always on the lookout for when sensorial materials, designed to heighten a sense and a refined awareness of the world, is misused. When this happens, we find a way to kindly remove the material and bring it back later with a fresh lesson. Otherwise misuse can spread and then the purpose or aim of the material is lost.

Suggested List for Creating the Culture Mastery Charts

The lessons in this list are only the basic activities for the sensorial *mastery chart* that will be presented to each child. You may want to expand it to include the stages of each key, or set of materials, for example including all three color boxes. But this basic list will help you keep the sensorial lessons balanced within this area, and with the other areas of the classroom work.

Visual

Cylinder blocks

Pink tower

Broad stair

Long (red) rods

Color tablets

Geometric cabinet

Constructive triangles

Knobless cylinders

Square of Pythagoras

Binomial cube

Trinomial cube

Aural or Auditory

Sound boxes

Bells (here or in the culture area)

Gustatory

Tasting bottles

Tactile

Sensitizing fingers

Rough and smooth boards

Graded rough tablets

Box of fabrics

Baric

Baric tablets

Thermic

Thermic bottles

Thermic tablets

Olfactory

Smelling bottles

Stereognostic

Geometric solids

Stereognostic bags

Mystery bag

Sorting grains

Blindfolded use of the cylinder blocks, pink tower,
broad stair, and long rods

MASTERY CHART, LANGUAGE

Language expresses the spirit of humanity in all its facets. Language is the means by which we can communicate the most intimate feelings. It is amazing to think that words written on a piece of paper by a person two thousand years ago, or two thousand miles away can move another person to tears, to anger, to any great emotion. This gives one the sense of wonder of the power of language.

Years ago, when I was a teacher of a 6-12 class in California, I read a poem by James Whitcomb Riley to a few of the students. It was a poem very close to my own experience as a child. In "Little Mandy's Christmas Tree" the poet tells the story of a poor family at Christmas. As I continued to read this long poem many other children joined us, because it was very different from the relatively privileged lives of these children. The first time I read it, I burst into tears toward the end and could not finish it, so one of the children had to read it for us. From then on, I was asked often to read this poem. It was amazing to the children that, even though the poem was written so long ago, and so far away from us today (Indiana), it had the power to force their teacher to cry. It inspired them to put their own emotions into their own writing.

Just as learning music does not begin with the Montessori bells, but depends on a lot of pre-bell preparation and experience, the same is true in learning language. The sandpaper letters are so well-known when one hears about Montessori schools, that there is a misconception that children are put in the primary class basically to learn to read and write and calculate. Nothing could be further from the truth. The goal of Montessori is the fulfillment of all of the aspects of a human being; curiosity and love of learning and work follow naturally, but they are a choice.

There is a lot of required work for the teacher who must have a deep knowledge of the subject area, of children, and of the methods of putting these two in touch with each other.

But, it is important to keep in mind that there is NO required work for children at this age. Everything in the primary class is offered, based on careful observation, and planning of the teacher. If a child has been given all of the pre-reading indirect and direct preparation lessons, and still does not learn to write and read at this age, there will still be plenty of positive learning experiences because of seeing other children enjoying writing and reading. That is excellent preparation for when a child decides to write and read. We focus on all of the aspects of preparation for the preparation; that is our job. The acceptance of offered lessons is the child's.

For years, when giving talks and workshops on language in the primary class, I have used this Pre-Reading chart that we received in my first teacher training course in London. This chart has been found to be helpful for many teachers. Rather than bemoaning the fact that a child is not writing and reading, we can look back at the direct and indirect preparation and offer lessons on these activities. Here are the details of this chart:

PRE-READING CHART

Increase in Vocabulary

(experience first, then corresponding language)

1 - Classified Cards

2 - "I Spy" Game

3 - News Time

4 - Sensorial Language

5 - General Language of the environment

6 - Poems, stories, songs, etc.

7 - "Logical Question" game

Preparation for Writing – Direct

Physical preparation:

1 - Metal Insets

2 - Sandpaper Letters

Intellectual preparation:

1 - Sandpaper Letters

2 - Movable Alphabet

Preparation for Writing – Indirect

Physical—Practical Life Exercises: general dexterity, with all exercises; control of the hand and arm, with the pouring exercises

Physical— Sensorial Work: movement of the wrist, with the geometric cabinet; lightness of touch, with the rough and smooth boards, and the knobbed puzzles; dexterity of fingers, with the cylinder blocks, and knobs on puzzles

Intellectual—the same list as with Increase of Vocabulary

1 - Classified Cards

2 - "I Spy" Game

3 - News Time

4 - Sensorial Language

5 - General Language of the environment

6 - Poems, stories, songs, etc.

7 – "Logical Question" game

Teachers and Parents as Writing Models

This was mentioned earlier in this book but it bears repeating. There is one more element in pre-writing that is very important, especially these days, when the statistics on reading and writing in many countries show that children are falling behind in this area. Children at this age are watching their family members and teachers and peers carefully. They want to learn to do what they see older children and adults in the home and school environment are doing. When children never see anyone reading a book, or writing with a pencil or pen, but instead looking at and tapping on some kind of electronic screen, it is the screen that is going to attract the child, not the book or the pen or pencil.

In the very first Montessori class in the slums of Rome, the *casa dei bambini*, Dr., Montessori spent many hours a day observing and learning from children. She took copious notes to ponder and organize in the evenings. I have often wondered if her modeling of handwriting had something, or a lot, to do with the fact that these children, who probably saw little handwriting in their homes, spontaneously began to write at age four, and easily began to read about six months later!

During the years that I was a Montessori classroom teacher I was constantly writing my observations on paper and the children saw me doing this. This, and probably the fact that all children entered my primary classes at age 2.5-3 and benefitted from the indirect and direct preparation activities, probably accounted for the fact that they all began to write spontaneously around age four, and to read around six months later. I am sure this is the case for many teachers.

Today children's records are usually kept on a computer and that may be necessary; but I believe it is very important that the original data, that the teacher records during class time, is recorded on paper with a pen or pencil. This is also something to share with parents for their own important roles as models in the home as we tell them the importance of being models of reading and writing in front of their children.

Suggested List for Creating the Language Mastery Chart

You can see that my own mastery chart items, listed below, followed the chart, adding more specific lessons from my language album:

PRE-READING:

Classified cards (naming)

Sensorial material language

Free Oral Expression (logical question game, news time, stories, poems, the "I Spy" or other sound games)

Metal insets

Sandpaper letters

Movable alphabet

Reading

Object box 1

Objects box 2

Puzzle words, group 1

Reading folders – reading booklets

Reading folders – sorting, 2 folders, 3 folders, etc.

Phonogram dictionary

Puzzle words, group 2

Classified cards - names

Classified cards – definition stages

   (Word Families)

Masculine/feminine

Singular/plural

   (Function Games)

Article game

Adjective game

Logical adjective game

Detective adjective game

Conjunction

Preposition

Verb

Adverb

Logical adverb game

Other verb games

   (Link between function games and reading analysis)

Command cards

   (Reading Analysis – Folders of sentences to cut up, 2 boards, symbols)

Subject and object (folders 1 and 2)

Extensions of the verb (folders 3 and 4)

Adjuncts (folder 5)

   (Free Composition)

Writing letters

Spelling

Capital letters

Placement on a line

Placement on a page (margins)

Written question game

Punctuation

(Application of Reading)

Use of book corner

Use of dictionary

Use of simple encyclopedia

Stories - read and told

Poems - read and told

MASTERY CHART, MATH

One year, while consulting with a school in Nepal, I was purchasing something in a shop when the electricity went off. Neither the high school student who was with me, nor the young lady at the check-out counter, could do the simple math needed to figure out my change. They could not do it in their heads or even on paper. This really helped me understand the importance of a certain level of math mastery even in the modern world of phone apps and computers.

But more than the practical aspect, when math is offered, and not required, in the Montessori way, it is really enjoyable. When a child enjoys learning something, more time is going to be spent working on it, and it is much more likely that the learning will be retained. According to Montessori theory, some of the main human needs and tendencies include just those skills that are necessary in order to enjoy, and master, math in the Montessori primary class. These are abstraction, calculation, order, movement, repetition, concentration, work, exactness, and perfection. The Montessori math materials, which have been used all over the world for over one hundred years with great success, provide for all of these. Through practical life the child has already experienced many examples of these human needs and tendencies. Now these physical and mental skills carry over into the math area.

Let us consider the interest in calculation, that is seen early in life, as an example. The abilities necessary to do a calculation are:

1 - Discrimination – which is aided by all of the work with the sensorial material

2 - Recognizing similarities – used in all of the pairing work with sensorial materials

3 - Observing differences – used in building the pink tower, red rods, and all grading exercises

4 - Recognizing a progression within a series, and having the ability to bring about order – aided by working with the color tablets, cylinder blocks, all grading exercises

5 - Appreciation of relationships – aided by work with the geometric solids, constructive triangles, and other sensorial material

6 - Comparing and contrasting series – work with the knobless cylinders

Math Materials

Practical life, cultural, and language materials must, for the most part, be created by the teacher. Sensorial and math materials can be purchased and just put on the shelves. This sometimes results in a classroom with only sensorial and math materials—yes, I have seen such classes. Just as with the language materials, there is much work that comes before math, and without it, when children are being taught math too early or when unprepared, the results are not good. Here are the general ages for math materials:

Age 4 – number rods, sandpaper numbers

Age 4.5 – number rods and symbols, spindle boxes, counters and cards, fractions, introduction to the decimal system, function of the decimal system, formatting complex numbers, teen boards, ten boards, 100 chain, 1000 chain (4.5 – 5.5), skip counting forward and backward (4.5 – 5.5), fractions

Age 5 – beads and cards addition (4.5-5), subtraction (5), multiplication (5), division (5-5.5), then positive snake game, positive strip board, tables with bead bars, multiplication board, unit division board

Age 5.5 – stamp game addition and subtraction, dot game, addition charts 3-4-5-6, subtraction charts 2-3, multiplication charts 3-4-5, division charts 1-2, maybe short bead frame

Age 6 – short bead frame, short division with the test tubes, stamp game – multiplication and division, hierarchies, long bead frame

Forced Math Work

I once was a substitute for a primary teacher's maternity leave for a short time. The child of the owner of the school was in my class. The owner insisted that I continue to require the child to work on the long bead chains, skip counting each day. She was certainly correct in thinking that during this "absorbent mind" period of life, children can actually "absorb" the multiplication tables easily, even memorizing them, when working with this material. Perhaps the owner of the school had experienced the typical trauma of memorizing multiplication tables as a child, and wanted to protect her child from this experience. But, what I observed right away, was that the child already hated working with the long chains! She dreaded it and could not concentrate. In our conversation, her Montessori-trained mother understood that this was not the way to learn math. Just as with writing and reading, even if a child does not master everything in these areas, it is more important that the work that is undertaken is enjoyed, and that the child is surrounded by other children enjoying all of the work.

Story Problems

Just as language is being carried out all day, casually, learning the specific vocabulary of the environment in conversations, and the formal language of poetry and songs, math can be part of a casual conversation. For example, "There are three crackers on the snack table. If one falls on the floor, how many will be left?" These can be a lot of fun, even funny.

Visiting a class of a teacher who had had the same training in London as I, I was interested to observe a math activity that was new to me. The teacher made up a story problem each day and wrote it on the blackboard. Here is an example "Sarah had 12 grapes. She shared them with 3 other friends. If they shared the grapes equally how many grapes did each person have?" During the morning, I watched several children go up to the board, read the words, and stand and think for a few moments. By lunch time someone had solved the problem and written the answer on the board. There was no discussion, no praise, no question as to who had solved the problem; this just a normal part of the day.

The teacher told me after my observation that the only thing she had to be careful about was to be sure, over a period of time, to use the name of each of the children in the class in one of the story problems, so no one felt left out.

Suggested List for Creating the Math Mastery Chart

It is clear that there are more math lessons listed here than will fit on one chart. I suggest that you examine your own system for teaching within the math groups and list just the ones that lead you naturally into the following lessons. For example, you might just list "multiplication chart 3" because you always teach 3, 4, and 5 to a child in the same week. Or list "teen boards" only, because you automatically present them first with the numbers immediately followed by a lesson on both numbers and beads.

This list is not in order by age and stage of development, but by math group. You can decide the best way to create the mastery chart.

Math - group 1

Number rods

Sandpaper numbers

Rods and symbols

Spindle boxes

Counters and cards

Decimal system presentation, beads

Decimal system presentation, cards

Function of the decimal system

Practice with beads and cards

Addition-beads and cards

Subtraction-beads and cards

Multiplication-beads and cards

Division-beads and cards

Long division-beads and cards

Stamp Game addition, simple and dynamic

Stamp Game multiplication, simple and dynamic

Stamp Game division, simple, dynamic, long, with zero

Dot game

Short bead stair

Teens - with beads

Teen boards with numbers

Teen boards with beads and numbers

Ten boards with beads only

Ten boards with beads and numbers

Linear counting - 100 chain

Linear counting - 1000 chain

Bead board - other chains

Skip counting

Positive snake game

Positive strip board (chart 1,2)

Addition charts 3, 4, 5

Addition chart 6

Negative snake

Negative strip board (1st presentation)

Negative strip board (2nd presentation)

Subtraction chart 2

Subtraction chart 3

Tables with bead bars

Multiplication board

Multiplication chart 3

Multiplication chart 4

Multiplication chart 5

Unit division board

Division chart 1

Division chart 2

Math - group 5

Short bead frame

Hierarchies (1-1,000,000)

Long bead frame

Short division with test tubes

Fractions, experience, names, symbols, functions, equivalents

Wisdom from a NYC Traditional Teacher of the Year

I would like to share some insight of one of the most revolutionary educators in the American school system this century, John Taylor Gatto. For almost 30 years, he dedicated his passion for teaching in the New York City public school system. He received the honor of being named "New York State Teacher of the Year" for three years in a row, in 1989, 1990, and 1991.

Eventually, after twenty-six years, Gatto became frustrated with required traditional education. He began to research what education could be. Then he retired from teaching. Later that year he spoke at Carnegie Hall, which launched a career of public speaking in the area of school reform, speaking in all fifty states and seven foreign countries. During this time, he researched education widely and was a favorite speaker at education conferences, including those of homeschoolers.

Our family attended one of his lectures at our local university. One of the statements he made I shall never forget:

> *A person can learn all the foundational math, reading, and writing information they need in roughly 100 hours of study. Public school, on the other hand requires a whopping 25,000 hours for the same things. But why?*

We had a very interesting discussion with him after the talk. He had heard of Montessori of course and agreed that emphasis is placed on math and sciences in traditional education because these subjects are easily measured, easily graded. And that all too often the teachers assigned to teach these subjects are not passionate about them.

Easy measurement and grading are not the case with writing, speaking, developing skills at working with, helping, and teaching others, initiating independent research, following one's passions, and all of the other elements of a Montessori education.

Math and sciences are very important in today's world, but if the result is the creation of adults who despise, or have no interest in, either, instead of enjoying this and wanting to know more, the teaching methods have failed.

Math and sciences, the way they are taught in Montessori classes are successful because they are fun, practical, and explored independently and with friends. Thus, the concepts can be retained throughout life and can even make subsequent math courses more easily understood and enjoyed.

My Own Math Story

My father was a physicist who loved math. Because I was the oldest child he could hardly wait to share his excitement in using a slide rule, which was really an early analog computer, with me. But he did not know how to bridge the gap between what I was learning in school and what he knew. I was frustrated because I could not share his love of this subject.

My love of math came later and I was so glad to be able to share it with him. During my first Montessori diploma course, we learned how to assemble beautiful, colorful, wooden prisms of the bi-nomial and tri-nomial cubes. For a young child, these are exercises in matching colors, sizes, shapes. But as the lecturer explained the underlying significance of these materials, it was as if a lightbulb turned on in my brain! It was clear that math, geometry, and algebra were all brought together, made physical, in one piece of Montessori math materials. In the following years as a teacher at both primary and elementary levels, my love of math never dimmed.

In conclusion I would say that, just as with all of the other primary lessons, math as taught in the Montessori way can be just as exciting for children. This is because, in the primary class, all of the work is offered, the child left free to explore and master concepts from an inner drive. The purpose of all of the work in the primary class is to enjoy, to create a desire to do and learn more, and to become a happy, balanced, well-rounded, compassionate, human being.

THE TEACHER'S JOURNALS
OR DIARIES

*[The teacher] must acquire a moral alertness which
has not hitherto been demanded by any other system, and
this is revealed in her tranquility, patience, charity, and
humility. Not words, but virtues, are her main
qualifications.*

— Montessori, *The Discovery of the Child*

Personal Journal or Diary

As with all teachers, a Montessori teacher grows and matures, and can become a better and more complete human being, through work with children. Entering the classroom in the morning—where one must be ready to focus completely on the environment, one's assistant, each child separately, and the group as a whole—one must be able to leave everything else outside, and be ready and in the moment, in order to do this work successfully.

When I was taking my first Montessori diploma course in London over fifty years ago I learned how to meditate. Over the years there have been very few days that I have entered a classroom without having meditated. When I had not been able to prepare myself in this way I could easily tell the difference, and I worked especially hard so that this situation would not affect the children.

The personal journal or diary documents one's growth in regard to this work. It is very private and not to be shared as it is, in a way, a conversation of discovery with oneself. It can be a record of relationships with colleagues or parents, thoughts about the school schedule or staff meetings, one's mood at a certain point in time or being affected by outside influences. I wrote in this journal whenever it seemed helpful in getting to know myself, and I kept it at home

I recorded personal notes on my own thoughts and emotions because it is important for the teachers to observe, and learn about, themselves as they observe, and learn about, children. Examples:

I am cutting down on coffee.

I need to do more observing and not so many presentations this week.

This saying made me laugh, "our meetings are held to discuss problems that would not exist if we had fewer meetings."

Remember to see [child's name] completely new each morning, and forget about what happened the day before.

Daily Journal or Diary

This journal can be kept at school. It is not necessary to write much, just to be sure for a daily check. It can record when certain children are absent and how that might affect others. It is important to get into the habit of writing a bit at the end of each day. Eventually one sees patterns emerging.

Looking back over the months, I would learn a lot from such entries as "It was very rainy and windy today and the children seemed restless" repeated several times. It seemed a pattern and when talking to other teachers I learned that it was common. So, I would be sure to be even more of a model of calmness than usual when entering the class on a windy or rainy day.

Here are some typical examples directly from one of my teacher's journals:

> *10/3 All sandpaper letters presented, a few to each child of course*
>
> *10/4 Today was windy and the children were restless*
>
> *10/5 No false fatigue!!! (This was the first day that all children worked straight through the 3-hour work period with no typical restlessness, false fatigue, that had been occurring around 10-10:30)*
>
> *10/8 Over the weekend I changed all vocabulary card sets, 2-3 new pictures in each. Sara was the first to discover this, then several others.*
>
> *10/9 No false fatigue*
>
> *10/10 Four children are out with flu, a very disruptive day, quiet but restless. The children always seem to notice, and comment, when not everyone is here*

I recently found my record book from a new class I began in 1973, twenty-five children completely new to Montessori, age span 2.5-5.5. This was my very first year of teaching! I thought this might be interesting to include some of the entrees. In this case I wrote a lot, and it was very therapeutic as a way to process the beginning days, and to recall the advice in particular lectured during the teacher training course, in a less than ideal situation.

> *9/21, First day of school. There are only "toys" in the classroom, steps to freedom lessons going well, will have to bring new material in at a more rapid pace. Good day.*
>
> *9/23, Four students through the first stage of learning how the classroom works in three days, very*

good. For some students, the 9-3 day is too long so we are ending work at 1:00 for these children, and [my aide's name] is taking them to playground.

9/26, Individual work and concentration for almost one hour most mornings, then a 15-20-minute group, then another long individual work time, short group just before class ends, teaching things like walking around floor mats, putting material quietly on shelves and tables.

10/2, A new psychology student came to observe, wanted to interact too much with the children – chaos!

10/5, Mid-morning chaos caused by group snack! so . . . On Friday, I set out the poured cups of milk and a tray and crackers on the "snack table" with one chair, and invited the children to go one-at-a-time for snack. It worked beautifully without causing a major break in the class routine. I will set out snack table at the beginning of class till I have given lessons for the children to do it independently. Friday was the best day so far. Children are starting to be aware of approaching someone to talk to them instead of yelling, and walking instead of skipping and running across the room.

10/12, The youngest student's attention span increased to over an hour. [Child's name] still can only concentrate for 5-10 minutes at longest. Snack table set out, teaching individual snack, and clean up, working very well; several children do not even want snack. Individual work time has increased to 1.5-2 hours easily, 1-2 short small groups per morning at most. We will need more practical life next week. Hopefully this will eliminate the need for daily groups.

RECORDKEEPING SCHEDULE BY THE DAY, WEEK, AND YEAR

There is so much to do as the teacher of a Montessori primary class: constant creation and re-creation of the environment, working with an assistant to make the best use of their skills and natural abilities in supporting the teacher, communication with the parents of one's students, and then there is one's own life away from school! If you are a new teacher, or perhaps preparing to sign a teaching contract, I hope this book will help explain to the administration the need for time spent outside classroom for your work.

So far in this book we have touched on the areas to be covered in creating the environment, a method of tracing the concentration of each child and the class as a whole, a way of covering all areas of learning, planning presentations for each child, recording mastery, and the private teacher's journal.

But how do we accomplish all of this? This depends a lot on the school and family life of the teacher. Is Friday afternoon the best time for you to sit down and think and write? Is early morning of each day better? Do you need to cover all of this work at the school or do you have a home office or space? Just as each child has an inner guide to follow when given the freedom in a prepared environment, the adult, the teacher, has an inner guide to be listened to in planning all of this work.

The rest of this chapter presents the system I personally developed in order to manage all of this. Some of these ideas have been mentioned earlier in the book, but here is a summary. Remember, these are just suggestions. The most important thing to remember is that recordkeeping should be something the teacher can look forward to, and enjoy.

Daily Recordkeeping

Teacher's Daily Journal or Diary

I didn't always write in this journal every single day, but most days. On very busy days I forced myself to do this each day by telling myself that I only needed to write two lines. Often this was enough—just the date and two lines. Sometimes those two lines opened the floodgates, and it became easier to write more.

Weekly Lesson Plan

I kept two clip boards with the weekly lesson plan and a pencil on the top of a set of shelves, (above the eye-level of the children in order not to be distracting), somewhere near the center of the classroom. It is important to have this in easy reach, so one can refer to it, and write on it, constantly throughout the day.

When you see a child at a momentary loss for something to do you can quickly look at the weekly lesson plan, checking the list of 3-4 or more lessons you have recorded after this child's name.

If you see that a child is attempting an activity but it is clear that a new presentation is needed, this is where you make a note to yourself to give another presentation to this child later, perhaps the following week, definitely at a neutral moment so it does not feel like a correction.

If you see that a child has begun to work on something, and is working on it in the correct way after having observed another child, this is a valid lesson so you record this as a presentation or lesson that has been given.

When it is clear that a child has mastered an activity, this is where you record this information to later be transferred to the appropriate mastery chart.

Notes:

Sometimes I sat on the observer's chair with one of the clipboards and had a look around at what each child was working on to record on the weekly lesson plan page. I was never disturbed when doing this because the children had learned that sitting on the observer's chair was important work, not to be interrupted.

Concentration Graph

I recorded the name of the child and the date on a blank concentration graph each morning. At the end of the day I filed this in the recordkeeping book, in the section for that child. When a concentration graph had been created for each child in the class I created a concentration graph for the class as a whole. Then I filed that in the back of the notebook.

Weekly Recordkeeping

Teacher's Personal Journal

Described in the last chapter.

Filling in Mastery Charts

This means taking the weekly lesson-plan page and filling in what each child has mastered over the last week. It means looking at every mastery chart—steps to freedom, practical life, cultural subjects, sensorial, language, math—and then recording: (1) a child has had the lesson, or (2) a child has mastered the lesson.

Creating the Weekly Lesson Plan for the following week

I did this at the same time as I was filling in the mastery charts. I had in hand the last week's weekly plan. I had in front of me all of the mastery charts.

Referring to albums/folders, and practicing new lessons (alone or with another adult)

One usually does not get through all of the lessons in one's teacher training albums, in all areas, each year. There will come a time when a child is ready for a lesson the teacher has never given. How do we prepare for giving this lesson? One of the most valuable parts of AMI teacher training is the hundreds of hours one spends in the *practicals* rooms (complete environments with all of the materials) giving lessons to other adults. During the required practice hours, there is always a very experienced Montessori teacher overseeing the practice, there to answer questions as they arise. Later, as teachers, we are lucky to have another adult to practice giving the lessons to. If not, we pretend there is an adult sitting next to us, and practice each step of the lesson before giving it to a child.

I have consulted in many schools where the teachers have not had this kind training experience and I can only imagine how difficult it is for them. Some teachers, out of necessity in some countries, have only been able to learn from teacher-training albums that they had purchased instead of being able to create themselves; which is difficult because it is the creating of albums that is the first step in learning the theory and materials. Many teachers have never had the opportunity to practice giving lessons to other adults under supervision of experienced teachers and must constantly refer to the written down lessons and then practice on the children. I know this is necessary sometimes and it makes me feel extremely fortunate that I had the training that I did. I hope this chapter will encourage these teachers to practice giving lessons to adults, over and over, until the lesson is learned.

But there can even be problems with the very best of training. One year I was working with a school in the beginning weeks, with a new teacher with an AMI diploma, but no teaching experience. I noticed that she almost ignored the child she was giving the lesson to; the child was looking around the room, not paying any attention to what the teacher was doing or saying. This did not inspire the child to do anything with the material after the lesson. I had never seen anything like this before, but I understood after talking to this woman's teacher trainer. During the training, the student said she preferred to practice alone with the materials rather than giving practice lessons to another adult. Practicing alone before giving a lesson is valuable, but when we practice giving lessons to another adult, and watching for the responses, we are clearly better prepared to give lessons to children.

Another time, when I was working on AMI primary courses in Thailand and Morocco, I noticed that some adults in training preferred to work on their own, and I was able to refer to the above example to explain that this is not an effective way of preparing to give a lesson to a child. Also, I saw that some of the teachers-in-training preferred to always give the lesson to the same person. In observing this situation, I could see that, just like an old married couple who know what each other is thinking and can almost finish each other's sentences, the same thing was happening in this practice. So, I explained to these teachers-in-training that when one is in a real classroom, having invited a child to a lesson, there is often no way to know how that child is going to react. One needs to be ready to make eye contact, or not make eye contact, depending on the child; one needs to be prepared to use language that is correct for that child's stage of language development; one needs to be aware of not moving and speaking at the same time so the child can focus on one or the other, watching the teacher's movements or listening to the words. One must be prepared to move even more slowly than usual for one child, and to be ready to repeat more often for another, and there are so many other variables.

As a result of hearing this, these teachers-in-training were able to step out of their comfort zone of working always with a friend, and the value became obvious very quickly, because there already was a need to adapt a lesson to the new person receiving the lesson.

For those who have had the experience of supervised practical sessions, it can be helpful when going back to an album and selecting a new lesson, to practice with another adult, and at the very least to practice the lesson alone in great detail.

Annual Recordkeeping

New term or semester six-week plan

Make a first six weeks plan, for either new or a continuing class, preparing the environment, and planning lessons that may not have been covered in the last term. Create a balance of all areas.

Updating mastery charts

Sometimes it is necessary to prepare new, or redo old, mastery charts. It may sound daunting to think about completely redoing the mastery chart for each subject, but I found it a satisfying way to look through the year's work in detail, and to get inspired for the coming year.

Updating record books

Prepare or redo the record books described in this chapter. The same value as updating the mastery charts. This work gives one a great review.

Teacher's continuing education

Go over the *general knowledge* book and make a plan to learn more about famous people for example, putting together simple stories that would be of interest to this age so you can tell stories. Study different kinds of art, artists, musicians, poets; learn more about flower corollas, leaf attachments, etc., so you have this knowledge solid and can share it with the children during this or the next year. The need to keep growing and learning as an adult is one of the joys of being a Montessori teacher.

The book *The Red Corolla, Montessori Cosmic Education* (for ages 3-6) is a great resource for growth of the adult as it includes the chapters in the section "The Work of the Adult": *General Knowledge, Leaf Collection, Formal Language.*

Additional Observation and Recordkeeping Suggestions

The following systems were presented to me during my AMI primary teacher training course. Even though I found the basic methods explained above—weekly lesson plan, concentration graphs, daily teacher's journal, and practicing giving lessons to adults before children—the most helpful if there is no opportunity for further recordkeeping.

The following methods are very helpful in our work; some years I used some of them and some years I used all of them. It can depend on how much space one has, such as teacher's storage or even a teacher work room, at a school, or if one must keep recordkeeping charts and books at home. You will develop what is best for you, deciding to incorporate some or all in your own observation and recordkeeping system.

Progress reports for each individual child

(and concentration graphs)

I kept these in a three-ring notebook with a section for each child. It is a dated, running list of notations. I found that I required just a few sentences on the emotional, physical, intellectual, social development, or anything else that stands out at any time.

This was done twice a month at least, but often I found that writing a bit about each child had become a regular part of my Friday (or Thursday if Friday was going to be impossible) routine. It helped me keep my attention on those children who are always working diligently and quietly off in the corner of the room, and not just those who needed more of my attention. Here I would record a child's special interests, what children they might be receiving lessons from or giving lessons to, overall health and condition of a child.

Examples might be "Sandra and Sarah who avoided each other for all of last year have suddenly become best friends" or "Tom's mother is on a business trip and he keeps asking me for hugs. I'm here." or "Alex turns everything into a gun. I must ask his parents if they know where this is coming from."

These are very private notes, just for the teacher to look back on to follow the child's progress. But sometimes they were very helpful in parent conferences as I looked at the concentration graphs of a child, the main focus of a conference.

I kept these records in the section of the notebook where I kept the concentration graphs for each child. That way it was easy to go to a child's section and see the concentration progress by looking at several concentration graphs all in the same place.

Individual subject plans

Again, I used a three-ring notebook with a section for each subject. Just as for the individual child this was a running list that I made from looking through my teacher-training albums. It helped make discoveries, for example, that I had presented a lot in one area during a particular month, but not enough in some other areas. For

113

example, I might have presented a lot in the physics area, but not taught any new poems or songs for several weeks. It helped keep my lessons to the children balanced, but it also helped to keep each section of the curriculum alive and new throughout the year.

Each week I made a list with something new from each subject, looked up the lessons in my albums and practiced them if necessary. I made sure all of the necessary materials were available. This sheet might have items not found in the mastery charts, for example, if there is to be a guest musician visiting the class, or if it is time to change the colored papers on the art shelves to reflect a coming holiday.

I kept this one-page list of suggestions on the same clipboard(s), underneath the weekly lesson plan sheet and referred to it when necessary.

Communication with Teachers of Entering
or Leaving Children

Transition from a home or infant community, and transition to a traditional school first grade or Montessori 6-12 class requires communication with the last or next teacher, and parents in order for the path to be smooth for the child, the family, the school. There is a lot of research and advice from experienced teachers for how to facilitate a smooth transition.

For example, originally it was thought that a child should stay in the infant community until age three. Over the years it has become clear that age 2.5 is usually better because at this age a child often outgrows what is available in an infant community and can become bored and troublesome. In some schools, a child in an infant community is able to move freely, as often as possible, to the primary class, then it becomes clear when the child is ready to be a permanent part of the new class.

Just as important is a discussion about a child in the primary class moving to the elementary class. Although the experiences in a primary class prepare a child for an elementary class in many ways, the primary class is not meant as merely a preparation for the elementary class. The purpose is to give the child a complete and happy primary class experience. Sometimes, it is possible for the child to visit regularly and then decide when to stay.

The most important consideration is, whenever possible, base the move on the needs and comfort of the child, not a certain or school year schedule. This is ideal and not always possible, but it is important to always consider the needs of a child first.

Children's Personal and Emergency Information

Emergency information must be kept within easy reach of the teacher, the assistant, and also the administrator at all times! There should be a log book to record any accidents, such as a bump on the head that could be serious. Report who witnessed it, who responded to it, how, when and who reported it to a parent and what was the result. And when and why a child might have been sent home for illness.

Somewhere you keep the legal records, attendance records, dated information about interactions with authorities, certification form copies. It is also where you keep private records of what you have learned about children that might affect their life in the class, such as birth order, ages of parents and siblings, who cares for the child, availability of the parents to the child, financial position of the family, exposure to culture etc. It is a good idea to have all this in one place in case you need to get to it quickly. If there is an office in the school a copy should be kept there for other staff to access in an emergency.

GENERAL KNOWLEDGE BOOK

In the beginning of our primary course in London, each of us constructed our own general knowledge book. This was an inspiration for rounding out our personal knowledge of the world. We laughingly called it "minding the gap" because "mind the gap" is a common warning on the London underground. In this case the *gap* refers to the space between the platform and the edge of the train, and one must be careful to step over it correctly.

Many years later I gave the same lectures and assignments in this area for the first AMI primary diploma course in Morocco. These lectures, along with pictures and some details can be found in the book *The Red Corolla, Montessori Cosmic Education* (for age 3-6). Here is an outline for beginning your own general knowledge book:

Geography

Section One: Continents, one country for each

Pick one country from each continent—Asia, Africa, North America, South America, Australia (or Australasia), Europe, and Antarctica if you like, but this last one is not necessary. Research and create one page for each with a few paragraphs of information that would be interesting to children, including: The physical geography (land and water form examples, temperature, etc.); Flora and fauna; The food eaten and how it is made, including interesting information about preparation and consumption of food; The people and how they look or dress; Culture, language, alphabet, architecture, art, music, religions, celebrations, artifacts, etc.

Make a collection of pictures for each of these countries and find or draw/paint illustrations of the flag of each of these countries.

Section Two: Flags, Countries, Capitals

117

Pick several of the most known countries from each continent and draw or paste in the flags, and list the names of the capitals. Sketch a map of each continent labeling the countries you have selected. Eventually you will record and learn all of them as you work with the puzzle maps with children.

Section Three: Land and Water Forms

List and illustrate the following land and water forms: *Island, lake, isthmus, strait, cape, bay, peninsula, gulf.*

For each one list seven examples, and be able to locate them on a map.

Examples: "Cape" - Cape Mendocino (California), Cape Horn (South America), Cape of Good Hope (Africa), Cape St. Mary (Madagascar), Cape Comorin (India), Cape Farewell (Greenland), North Cape (Scandinavia)

Biography

It was difficult to do this research in London at that time, and almost impossible to find female examples, examples of famous people of a variety of races, and examples from the various countries represented in our student body.

This is certainly different today, so be sure to find examples, in all five sections of the biography general knowledge section, of all sexes and many countries, certainly the country where you are or will be teaching. Today we are very fortunate for when we are with the children we will find that there are many children's books with pictures and interesting information depicting the lives of famous people.

Biography Section One: Poets

List seven poets from various centuries, especially from the country where you are or will be teaching. Research them and record their birth and death years and interesting information about their lives and poetry. This is not encyclopedia or Google information that is interesting to adults, but details about the person's life and work that would be interesting to a child of primary class years. Record at least one poem for each. My first ones were Basho, John Milton, Edward Lear, Emily Dickinson, William Blake, William Wordsworth, and Lord Byron. Here are two examples of poems that my children loved (I only taught the first verse). Children in my class loved these poems and did not even notice that some of the vocabulary is probably out of range of most adults, as many words are new to children at this age:

The Tyger, by William Blake
Tyger, tyger, burning bright
In the forests of the night,
What immortal hand or eye
Could frame thy fearful symmetry?

The Rainbow, by William Wordsworth
My heart leaps up when I behold
A rainbow in the sky:
So was it when my life began;
So is it now I am a man;
So be it when I shall grow old,
> *Or let me die!*
The Child is father of the Man;
And I could wish my days to be
Bound each to each by natural piety.

Biography Section Two: Composers

List seven composers from various centuries. Research them and record their birth, some interesting facts about their lives and music of interest to children. List their most famous or representational work. Collect a picture of each and a recording of a piece of music. I chose as my first seven that year: Claudio Monteverdi, Johann

Sebastian Bach, George Frideric Handel, Wolfgang Amadeus Mozart, Frédéric François Chopin, Ludwig van Beethoven, and Arnold Schonberg.

Biography Section Three: Artists

List seven artists, research them, recording their birth and interesting information about their lives and work. Go to museums and collect postcards of several examples of the work of each. My first artists were: Rembrandt van Rijn, El Greco, Jacques Louis David, Hokusai, Eugène Delacroix, Vincent Van Gogh, and Picasso. I selected them because their work really moved me in the museums in London. I collected postcards of many others, two of each, and used them all in class as 3-part language materials. In the course in Morocco the students found these pictures online. It is not illegal to use most online picture materials for one's own use.

Biography Section Four: Scientists and Inventors

List seven scientists from various centuries. Research them and record their birth and death years, and personal facts about their lives and inventions that would be interesting to children. If possible find pictures of them and their work. Mine were: Galileo, Sir Isaac Newton, Luigi Galvani, James Watt, Pierre and Marie Curie, and Guglielmo Marconi.

Biography Section Five: Authors

List seven writers from various centuries. Research them and record their birth, death, interesting information, and major or most interesting works. I researched: Rene Descartes, Charles Dickens, Lewis Carroll (Charles Lutwidge Dodgson), James Joyce, George Orwell, Jean Cocteau, and Allen Ginsberg.

Zoology

The five classes of vertebrates—fish, amphibian, reptiles, birds, and mammals—are featured for two main reasons. They can clearly be seen by children at this age; they form the basis for the Zoology work in the elementary class. Because this is the sensorial stage of development, we introduce children to those animals that they can see in their world, such as (fish) in aquariums; (amphibians) frogs and tadpoles in ponds; (reptiles) garden snakes and turtles in gardens; (birds) in the sky and on the branches of tree and on bird feeders; (mammals) farm animals and pets. Therefore, the sets of language cards for the five classes of vertebrates are always kept on the shelves, even though other sets of zoology cards (spiders, cats, dogs, butterflies, tide pool creatures, insects, etc.,) can be rotated in order to inspire the children to look carefully for what is on the shelves.

Zoology Section One: Mammals

Research between five and seven mammals. Find pictures. Record information that would be interesting to children such as their size, where they live, what they eat, if they are mentioned in literature (list poem). Write a little story for each, ideally from your own experience.

For an example, here is a story I recorded in my general knowledge book, that children loved hearing. It is a true story about a raccoon:

> *One evening a large raccoon came into our house in San Francisco, squeezing through the cat door. It sat still and looked at the bowls of cat food while our two cats just sat quietly and watched. Then the raccoon flicked the cat food out of one of the bowls with its paws, and into the water bowl before eating it. It was washing the food. When it was finished eating, the raccoon turned around and left, again squeezing through the cat door. Then the cats approached their bowls and continued their dinner.*

My mammals were: raccoon, sperm whale, striped skunk, porcupine, black bear, and buffalo. The pictures I collected were later made into cards to begin my first classified card set of mammals.

121

Zoology Section Two through Four:

Birds, Reptiles, Amphibian, Fish

Research 5-7 of each of these, just as was done with the mammals.

Botany

Botany Section One: Leaf Collection

Go to the botany leaf cabinet if you have access to one, and record the shape and name of 5-7 of the leaf shapes represented there. Then go out into the world and find an example that you can press. Later put this into your general knowledge book. Label it by the shape of the margin, and the name of the plant, the common and scientific name if possible.

It was very interesting to do this in a large city such as London. We discovered that some of the leaf shapes were only found in tiny weeds that were growing in the cracks next to a walkway.

Further botany sections

Finding the above leaves was just the beginning. Our "leaf collection" book contained information on the attachment of leaves to the stem, parts of the leaf, part of the root, part of the flower, types of corollas, types of roots, and much more. Use this section of your general knowledge book to sketch examples of the various botanical classifications you have learned on your course (or found in the *Red Corolla* book). Use this section of the general knowledge book to record drawings (pressed examples if you like) and names of all of the botanical classification you learned in your course, such as corollas, leaf attachments, types of fruits, varieties of roots, and so on.

Since we students had come to London from a great variety of countries we only began this part of our book with examples from

London. But this was our guide to do the same thing when we were back home. Then our students would be able to explore their own environment with many botanical concepts.

Botanical Language

Each specimen in botany will have a different common name but learning the scientific name will be much more interesting and valuable for a child at this age. For example, *dandelion*. The scientific name is *Taraxacum officinale*. This word may feel difficult for the adult who has not studied Latin to use, but it is as easy as any other word for a child. You could include (when making language cards) the French *dent de lion*, which means "the tooth of a lion", a very interesting story for children. In the elementary class students will learn much more about the scientific name and the classification of plants (and animals).

Today I have seen many situations where the use of the scientific name is only taught in the elementary class, but I always included it in the primary class, when children take in any vocabulary based on sensorial experience easily, because this is the absorbent mind period of life, the first six years.

As for the shapes of leaves. If we teach them the names of the plant for a particular leaf, that will of course be valuable. But if we give them the geometric shape keys of identifying leaves, their exploration and language will grow and grow. For example, the *orbicular* leaf shape is more or less round, an *orb*. Children will be able to find round leaves in garden plants, weeds, trees, with no help from us. And they will be able to express themselves, and share their discoveries, with the correct language. This is true scientific exploration and language.

I hope this research possibility inspires you as much as it did me all those years ago. Many years later, even though I am not in the classroom but have been working with parents and teacher in thirty countries, I have never lost my enthusiasm for learning more about

123

all of these subjects and this enthusiasm is contagious. The excitement that comes from the children who are given all these keys to the natural and human world has never gone from my memory.

FORMAL LANGUAGE BOOK

The label "formal language" refers to language that usually does not come up in one's daily life; this is the language of songs, fingerplays, poems, and stories. Since now is the absorbent mind stage of development, and the sensitive period for language, providing these is valuable both at home and in the Montessori primary class.

One year I was giving a workshop on this subject to primary teachers at a Montessori conference. At the end of the day, I passed around pieces of paper and told the teachers that if they would like to write down and turn in a list of their favorite, from their childhoods or teaching, in this area, I would collate them and send them to everyone who wanted the list. I was amazed to find that only a few teachers could come up with a list. It just had not been part of their childhoods, and so was not a part of their teaching.

During our teacher training course, we began our collections, our own formal language book. I kept mine in the classroom with me, because even though I eventually memorized many examples, my collection grew constantly over the years. The notebook was divided into sections: songs, fingerplays/action rhymes, poems, and stories.

Many of the favorites I laminated on cards, with an identifying picture at the top, so a child could select one and bring it to me or an older student, to read. There were picture books with songs, fingerplays, action rhymes, and poems in the classroom, usually the library or book corner. And when you notice that a particular poem or song, etc., is becoming a favorite of the children, add it to your formal language book.

Formal language Categories

Songs

I made photocopies of songs from books, so that I would have the melodies, piano music, and guitar chords at my fingertips. I was sure to include songs in other languages. My primary children knew at least one song each in Japanese, Hebrew, Spanish, French, Portuguese, and German, and I wish I could have had more languages represented. This is much easier today.

Fingerplays and action rhymes

A *fingerplay* is a poem that combines the spoken, or sung, word with matching actions carried out with the hands, and sometimes the whole body. These are very important because it is through the actions carried out, directed by the words, (as in "Itsy Bitsy Spider" or "Heads and Shoulders, Knees and Toes") that the child learns what the words mean, increasing vocabulary, and having fun.

Poems

As I expanded my knowledge of poets in the biography part of my general knowledge work, I added specific examples in the formal language book. Then each time I told a story about a writer or poet I could give more examples of their work. Quite often I was taught a new poem by one of the students, or the parents of a student. These went right into my collection.

Stories

Children's favorite stories are the little incidences that happened to us, their parents, and teachers, when we were children or even as adults. Just as children often prefer hearing their parents and grandparents tell stories to being read books before going to sleep at night, it is the same in class.

Here is an example of a story I used to tell:

> *One day we (I gave the names of the family members) were all sitting down to breakfast. (Sometimes I went into detail about the ambience of the situation, the*

126

food, who cooked, what we were all wearing, the sounds of
birds we might hear through the window, what the
weather was like, and other details, depending on the
reaction of the audience which was just one child or a
few). Suddenly a shadow fell across the table. We all
simultaneously (they loved learning this word) looked up,
and then our eyes were directed to the window just above
the kitchen table. And what do you think we saw (the
child/children always knew the answer to this questions).
To our great surprise we saw the lovely face of our horse,
Bonnie! She had figured out how to get out of the corral
and had come to find us.

I could tell that story many times, sometimes it being requested, because children love repetition, and knowing what was coming next. Keep stories like this in your book. I did, or I would not have been able to share it with you.

BEGINNING A NEW PRIMARY CLASS

Most of all, the children must be made to feel secure and confident in the environment. They need to know what will happen next during the day, to understand the procedures for arriving and departing school. Each child should have an individual welcome as they enter the classroom; you may decide that the assistant will be the one to greet the children as they arrive so the teacher can focus on what happens after the children enter the classroom. The beginning guidelines must be few and clear so the children learn that the teacher and assistant are kind and understanding authorities. If there is a change from outside to inside shoes as one enters a classroom, in the beginning a child may feel more comfortable keeping on the outside shoes, but this will gradually change as the child becomes more comfortable and sees what the others are doing. So, this is not a rule, but a point of arrival in understanding the classroom procedures.

There should be a compassionate agreement between teacher and assistant for possible problems with children in the first days. For example, if a child is crying, they should be comforted away from the group or others may become frightened.

The parents should be informed of all of these aspects of beginning school, and to understand that any communication with the teacher will take place at other times, that their child's happiness and security in beginning school is the priority. It is important to explain the importance of, for example, a jacket and shoes that a child can learn to manage independently, and for arriving at school on time (within an official 20 minutes or so arrival time) because of the young child's need for security in what to expect throughout the morning, throughout the day. I took attendance, silently on a paper kept with my recordkeeping papers, after the arrival period. Parents will understand when it is made clear that it is the happiness and comfort of their child that is the priority above all else.

My First Year Teaching a Primary Class

As I look back, my first year of teaching was not an ideal situation, but it was valuable in many ways in my growth as a teacher. I had completed the AMI primary diploma in London, England, and then returned to San Francisco, California, having been offered a position at the school where my daughter had been a primary student, and where I had discovered the Montessori method of education.

The school did not need a teacher, but wanting to take advantage of my training, a new class space was found in a church near the main school. There was always a waiting list of families wanting to enroll their children so the class was filled to capacity, twenty-five children from age two to six, attending for a full day from nine to three. Because the class was new, all of the children and most of the parents were new to the idea of Montessori.

One of the school observations during my training in London was that of a new class, in a similar situation. The class had been established two months before my observation. It was in a church hall where the shelves were turned to the wall at the end of each day for church functions. There were at least twenty children, a mixed age group, all new to Montessori. The non-teaching assistant calmly moved about straightening shelves and responding to questions of the children. Midmorning, the very experienced Montessori teacher and I sat down at one end of the classroom to observe, and one of the children asked us if we would like tea. The child then proceeded to make tea for us, bringing it on a tray with a flower in a small vase. After only two months, these children were working and happy.

I followed all of the advice from my training as closely as I could, much of it shared earlier in this book. But still, in the beginning there was a lot more movement and noise, sometimes chaos, than in the established classes in London that I had observed during my training. It was difficult for some of the children, and me, to concentrate.

However, even though I was a new, unexperienced, teacher, two months to normalization was my goal; I had seen it with my own eyes.

Splitting the class

After a few days, in order to create a more peaceful feeling and to be successful in the early lessons, my assistant and I split the class into two groups, each of mixed ages. We made two lists and as the children arrived the next morning, the "inside" children were invited to stay inside and select work, and the "outside" group sat together with the assistant for a short time, till all had arrived. Then this group walked around to the play area. I kept always the same group beginning inside and the same group beginning outside, in order not to upset the strong sense of order at this age.

The outside area was less than optimum and there was no possibility of accessing the outside area directly from the classroom; it was not possible to have free-flow inside to outside, or to take work outside. The children had to walk on a city sidewalk, in a group, with an adult, to move between the classroom and the outside area. And there were only a few toys and climbing possibilities. Still, I had decided that it was necessary to split the group like this for a short time. Midmorning, after about 1.5 hours, the assistant brought the children in and led the other group to the outside area.

This was a wise decision; it made all the difference. There was, for each short morning work period of a little over an hour, a mixed age group of twelve or thirteen children. The atmosphere was much calmer and quieter. I could concentrate more on the small group *steps to freedom*, practical life, and language lessons, and could give more individual lessons.

At noon, we gathered to have lunch together, unpacking lunch boxes, children choosing where to sit, conversing, cleaning up. Because the children, when in the two smaller groups, had grown used to a more calm and quiet atmosphere, now the lunch period and the rest of the day continued to be more peaceful.

As the lunch things were cleared away, the older children and my assistant set up eight-ten small cots in the darker end of the classroom taken from a stack of small folding cots, a requirement by the state of California for preschools at that time. From 12:30 or so until 3:00, we all stayed inside; the younger, or anyone who chose to, napping, and the others working.

We ended up splitting the group in the morning for about ten days, two weeks. Then one morning I welcomed each child with the news, in a quiet voice, that they could stay inside. They were all very glad to receive this news because they had begun to value the classroom work. The only outside time from then on was the few children who wanted to be outside for a short time after lunch, which they did with my assistant, but they preferred the classroom work.

Preparing the Environment

Do not have all of the materials out and available on the first day! In preparing a classroom for a new group of children, first I placed all of the materials on the shelves according to the plan I had made – all of the practical life, culture, sensorial, language, and math materials. Next, I took detailed photos of each area of the classroom, because most of the materials will be removed. Remove everything that should not be there on the first day. On that first day, most of the shelves will be empty but that is exciting, because the parents will have been told, and the children will gradually figure out, that a lot of wonderful material will be coming.

One of the reasons a Montessori primary class can function successfully is because "there is a place for everything and everything is in its place" (quoting my grandmother). So, when gradually adding materials to the shelves, I checked with photos and could be sure that each piece of material had its own place, and would belong there throughout the year.

Gradually over the first six weeks, depending on whether the children are new or experienced Montessori students, the teacher will gradually fill all or most of the shelves. As one brings materials in over time, it is important to keep the areas balanced.

Number and Ages of Children

Even though the morning of the split class was quieter, I observed that when the whole class were together, the increase in work inspired the children. They would often watch someone and then come to me and ask for a lesson. And the increase in incidences of teaching and helping among the children, independent of the adult, was so lovely to watch.

I have never been able, because of state floor space laws for preschools, to have a class of more than twenty-nine children, but I know that when the age spread is wide, and the number of children large, it is easier to teach. Montessori recommended a mixed age group of thirty to thirty-five children to one trained teacher, and one non-teaching assistant.

Traditional compared to Montessori ratio

When the teaching methods are traditional, the teacher giving the information to the children in groups, clearly a lower teacher: student ratio is valuable, and helps the teacher give a bit of individual help to each child. That is why we hear such teachers asking for small groups of children.

But in Montessori since it is the role of the teacher to put the children in touch with the environment for self-education, and to teach children how to teach and help each other, a higher ratio is very important.

However, the ratio that Montessori recommended only works if the teacher is well-trained, and either a natural or an experienced teacher. It is too much to ask of a teacher who, as is true all over the world, has only been able to learn to teach in a Montessori class from a short, or online, course, or from a book.

Other Ways to Introduce Children to a New Class

I have heard of many other ways to begin a new class, and only offer my experience as an example that worked for me. Although it is vital to have a mixed age group, sometimes a class will begin with just the older children for a few days, and then bring in the younger ones because the elders will be the models, the teachers, for the younger. Some teachers like to have individual children, with their parents, come to be shown around the class for a few minutes before the term begins. It does not suit every child to come for three hours, or full day, right away. Set different times for different children if necessary. Some bring in a few children, of mixed ages, at a time, every few days. No matter what is decided, it should be based on careful observation of how each child reacts, how soon the children feel comfortable, relaxed, safe, curious, and happy.

A Beginning Schedule and Lessons

Free work: As the children arrive they are invited to select a table mat or a floor mat, to lay this out on the floor or a table, and then choose something from a shelf, and place it on the mat. These are self-evident materials that need a very short lesson by the adult. You say, "This should be put this back on the shelf when you are finished." and you watch to see if each child needs help in managing to put the material and the mat back. Putting material away is NOT required and it may take some children longer than others to learn this. In the meantime, the adult is the model of graceful movement in putting these things away.

One of the lessons we give is how to carefully pick up and place a chair or stool, "tucking in" under the table when an activity is completed. In a class where I was consulting and there were many new children, I observed that there were four or five chairs that had not been tucked in and were in the way. The teacher approached a young student, pointed the situation out and asked if the young boy would like to tuck in the chairs "for the children who had not learned to do this yet." The boy was glad to oblige and did a beautiful job of it; it was good practice for him and a lesson for all of the children who were watching him. A lovely example of teaching by teaching, not by correcting.

This "free work period" may last only half of an hour in the beginning,

Whole class group: Next the children can be gathered to sit on the floor with you (NOT on the "walking on the line" line!) for a song, finger play, talking about children's names. One of the games that I taught from the very beginning was this one: I would point to the ceiling and say, "Point to the ceiling!" and most of us would do that. They I might say something like, "Close your eyes!" and then "Put your hands behind your back." And so on. This is quite fun and it is one of the most valuable ways to get children into the habit of doing what the teacher says. Also, I referred to this game later when introducing the verb in the language work. The children referred to this as the "point to the ceiling" game and sometimes asked for it or played it among themselves.

Free work: Next, after maybe ½ hour or ¾ of an hour, excuse the children one at a time to return to choosing individual work.

Alternating free work and whole class groups: The morning at this point will consist of alternating individual work and whole group activities. The whole group activities can include a group visit to the bathroom to show how the toilet works and where and how one can wash hands (In Thailand there was a special lesson at this point on where to place one's *inside* shoes and put on the *toilet* shoes, that were only used in the bathroom). A whole group may be the time for a group snack. I preferred to include pouring activities early and so introduced individual snack table very early in the year where children could pour themselves a glass of water and have a piece of fruit or a cracker, and then clean up this simple activity.

Throughout the first weeks you will be amazed at the number of songs, fingerplays, and poems the children will memorize in these first groups. Truly an example of the absorbent mind.

Many grace and courtesy lessons can be acted out during these groups, such as taking turns shaking hands and saying "Good morning Samantha," (or whoever one chooses to approach and shake hands with) if that is part of your culture, practicing handing an object to another person and saying "Thank you," and "You are welcome," or picking up a stool and being challenged to place it back on the floor so slowly that it makes no sound as it touches the floor.

"Where does it belong?" was another game I played with the children in a new class, or with a group of new children in an established class. I invited the children close their eyes if they were comfortable with that, then I would very quietly go to a shelf, pick up a piece of material, carry it back and quietly place it on a floor mat in the middle of the group. "Okay, open your eyes. Does anyone remember where this belongs?" Then a child would pick up the material and put it away. This is very easy to do in the beginning of a new class because there are very few pieces of material and they are all on the same set of shelves. At first, I put the floor mat down right next to these shelves, and gradually moved the mat, and the game, further and further from the shelf of these first toys. This opened the children's eyes to the larger classroom space and was wonderful experience in walking, carrying objects, learning where all of the materials belonged, and putting materials away.

Another grace and courtesy lesson is to have the children help you quietly move a few tables and chairs out of the way, then place several floor mats close to each other on this cleared space creating a kind of "maze". The challenge is to walk from one end of the maze to the other without touching a floor mat with one's foot. Make it easy at first and then more and more difficult to do this. This is one of the best lessons I have found to teach, not only careful movement, but to give practice in not interrupting a child who is busy concentrating on work on a floor mat.

As the days and weeks pass there will gradually be longer and longer free choice, uninterrupted concentration, work periods and fewer groups. Beware of becoming stuck in a pattern or schedule of having groups. We must be constantly aware of the importance of each child's growing independence. This is a very subjective plan to be modified depending on the maturity of the children in the new class,

Introducing new material

In these first weeks, as you bring new material in to the class, in the beginning, show all of the children the material in a group, give them the name, and show them where it goes on a shelf. Individual lessons on the use will follow in the work periods. You could play the "where does it go" game after several new thigs have been brought in.

A reminder from Montessori

One day, a few years after I had been teaching primary classes, I assigned myself to re-read all of Montessori's books, and to pull out all of the references to "collective lessons" (sometimes called "circle time" or "group" today). I found several references, but all were in the parts of her books where she was writing about the traditional way of teaching with groups. In each case she was clear "collective lessons" belonged in the traditional class, but that this is not the way lessons are given in a Montessori class. It was reassuring to be reminded.

Freedom comes gradually

It is always easier to keep the children close to you in the beginning and to gradually give more and more freedom, than the other way around; it is extremely difficult to make order when one gives too much freedom when children don't know what to do with it! The children gradually learn to be independent, and able to handle more and more freedom of choice in activities

Plan small group lessons into four or five developmental groups

Along with the few whole-class group lessons, make lists dividing the children into several different developmental groups, roughly based on age, but also on development. Have suggested individual and small group lessons for each of these groups and have them at your fingertips, on the weekly lessons plan, for reference during the day. The first group lessons will be the "steps to freedom," then language, then practical life, then cultural, language, and math.

The first day there should be enough link-to-home toys for each child to have one. The teacher demonstrates, in small or whole class groups, how to use a floor or table mat; how to pick up, carry, place on a table or on the floor, roll or fold, put back. The same with toys and early practical life materials.

Sometimes I made a game of having everyone close their eyes while one child selected a toy and put it on the floor mat in the middle of the group, then another raised their hand and tried to quietly put it back where it belonged. All of the toys were a set of shelves near the entrance to the classroom so the children could see all of the materials being used. They could easily identify where on the shelf (the only empty space) the toy belonged. It was a good way to make the point that everything has its own place.

It can be a matter of days, or sometimes weeks, that many of the children will no longer need to be gathered into small groups, but eventually there will be an environment filled with independently working children, all happily concentrating, thriving, during the uninterrupted three-hour work period.

Is Montessori Too Strict? Too Permissive?

Questions like this are typical when a new class is being established. It is well to be prepared. Montessori has been sometimes described as too strict, but on the other hand it has been described as too permissive. In reality, it is a balance of both, the teacher is strict where this is helpful, and permissive when the children are ready to handle the freedom. The system of beginning a new class, as described here, moving gradually from dependence on the adult to independence, is a perfect balance. Every step explained and recommended in this chapter is for the good of the children, and I hope it will enrich your own teaching experience.

THE FIRST SIX WEEKS
OF A CONTINUING CLASS

One year I was visiting a Montessori class on the last school day before summer; the teacher and the assistant and all of the children were on the playground instead of in the class. I asked if this was a decision by all of the children. I was told that, no, several of the children had wanted to stay inside, but the teacher thought being outside would be a treat. She thought that there was no sense in giving lessons at the end of the year because the children would forget everything over the summer.

Since then I have learned that this is not the case. A lesson that is given to a child at the end of Friday afternoon is often the first thing the child goes to on Monday morning. The lessons given on the last day before summer are, likewise, the work a child is most interested in when school begins. The brain seems to be working on the concepts over the break. So, the first thing to think about in planning for a new semester, is to prepare the environment and give the lessons up until the last moment before the end of the year. And then, when school begins, observe to see if there is a difference in what the children choose to work on.

In the United States, most schools have a fall term and a spring term and a long summer break. In other places, there are three terms with only a month break between them. Some schools have year-round school with the children in classes with a Montessori teacher while some have year-round school, but with adults without Montessori training in charge of the children during the summer or term breaks. These differences need to be taken into account when preparing for the beginning of a Montessori school term.

First Days

Depending on how many children are going to be there for the first days, and what their experiences have been over the break, it might be possible to just shake hands and say "hello" (or whatever the greeting is in your country) to most of them as they get back to work. However, if some are new, you might look through the last chapter on beginning a new class and benefit from some of these suggestions. Many schools prefer to have the returning children come on their own on the first days, especially if any changes have been made in the environment, so the older children are back to work, and good models, when the new children enter.

Ages of Entering Children

In my own school, we had a long summer break. A week after the returning children were settled in the new children came. There were twenty-nine children (limited by law because of our floor space per child) from the ages of two to seven years. By the second year of the school being in operation, we had a waiting list, so we accepted only young children, so they could benefit from the complete 3-5-year cycle. This was excellent for the individual children and for the whole class.

The two-year-olds entered, no more than one or two at a time, in the fall, or during the year near their second birthday. They were like new family members coming into a family of calm, busy, kind, and nurturing, older siblings who had been there for two, three, or four years and who took thoughtful and gracious care of them.

Ratio of Adults to Children

As I said in the last chapter, one of Dr. Montessori's most interesting discoveries was that a primary class worked best, when the teacher was well-trained in a course that met Montessori's standards, if there were 30-36 children, one teacher, and one nonteaching assistant.

Sometimes I hear people say that our children are different today, unable to handle these numbers, but I think the poor and hungry, wild children of the San Lorenzo slum had their own problems, such as hunger and being without parents all day long. There will always be problems, but the Montessori recommendations of ratio of adult to children has proven successful now for over a hundred years, all over the world, in many different situations.

Sometimes in my international work I have seen more adults than this in a classroom, for example if two or more languages are being taught, and sometimes this seems to work, but not often. But if you have the possibility to follow Montessori's recommendation, I think you may be pleasantly surprised at the results.

The Schedule

I found that a half-hour arrival time, from 8:30-9:00 was relaxing for all concerned, including the parents. Then a three-hour uninterrupted work time till noon. If possible another work period, as long as possible, in the afternoon. It is very important to explain to the parents the importance of that three hours so they do not bring children after 9:00.

In one school where I was a consultant, the three hours were repeatedly interrupted because parents did not understand why they had to be on time; they were being very casual about the time they dropped off their children. This is natural perhaps in a traditional preschool, but not in our schools.

This school solved the problem in two ways. They focused on helping the parents understand the reason for the three-hour work period and the value of concentration, and in those few instances that this was not enough, the classroom door was locked after arrival time. The parents had to be taken to the office and ask a staff member to bring them to the class.

When parents understand that deep concentration, and the resulting happiness and kindness, is valued over anything else, they definitely want this for their children.

MOVING TO A NEW ENVIRONMENT

My own school began in an upstairs room, in an empty wing of a Catholic school in Petoskey, Michigan. The number of children allowed in this space was limited by law to nineteen children. We began with three children, and by the end of the semester had nineteen and a waiting list. Fortunately, we were able to purchase a little house so more children could attend.

We were moving from a traditional one-room class in a large brick building, with high ceilings and one wall lined with shelves and windows, to a little house with several rooms opening on to each other. There was a kitchen/breakfast room, bathroom, living/dining room, large entrance room for changing clothes—essential in a place where there are often six months of snow during the school year—a bit clumsy access to the outside, and a half of a flight of stairs going down to a landing where the children could have a seat and quietly observe a new aviary of ring-necked doves, and finally a place for a piano!

In planning how to arrange the new environment, I took to heart the strong need for order exhibited by children at this age. They were used to knowing exactly where every piece of materials belongs on which shelf in the classroom. I put a lot of thought into the arrangement of the different areas—practical life, culture, sensorial, etc.—attempting to create something as logical as the arrangement the children were accustomed to. The parents and older children helped with the transporting of furniture and materials and some of the arranging, so moving, we hoped, would not be such a shock. We moved in the middle of the year. On the first day in the new place, even though there would be new students because we had more space, I had only the returning children come, because I knew that it was essential for them to be able to function in this environment, to be able to find items they wanted. Their comfort, and ability to work and concentrate, were going to be the model for the younger children.

However, halfway through the first morning, a little girl who had been with me since the day the school opened two years earlier, and who was always busy and happy and concentrating—and who had participated, along with her parents, in the move—came to me with tears in her eyes, lamenting, "I can't find anything to do!"

It was the same for all of the children, they had to find everything and reestablish their awareness of the new space before they could function.

Many years later, a friend Montessori teacher was planning a similar move of her primary class, from one room to a space with several rooms. The move was going to take place in the beginning of the fall term. When I shared my experience with her she decided to include the older children in the move and arrangement of the class. One difference was that, rather than giving the returning students some days to get used to the new environment before beginning the new little ones, she welcomed old and new students on the same day. A big mistake. Chaos reigned because there were no good models of returning students who knew how to navigate the new environment.

There is no one-size-fits all in planning the move of an established class to a new space, but hopefully sharing these two experiences will offer a little help for teachers, administrators, parents who might be contemplating a move.

Nature endows a child with a sensitiveness to order. It is a kind of inner sense that distinguishes the relationships between various objects, rather than the objects themselves. It thus makes a whole of an environment in which the several parts are mutually dependent. When a person is oriented in such an environment, they can direct activity to the attainment of specific goals. Such an environment provides the foundation for an integrated life.

What good is there in an accumulation of various objects if they are not arranged according to some order? This would be like having furniture without a house in which to put it. One who knows various objects but does not understand their mutual relations is like one living in a state of chaos from which one cannot extricate oneself.

It is in childhood that one learns to guide and direct oneself on the way of life. The first incentive is given by nature in the sensitive period that is connected with order. Nature is like a teacher who gives the class its first notions of geography by furnishing them with a plan of the classroom.

  – Montessori, *The Secret of Childhood*

PARENT COMMUNICATION

Since I was already a mother when I discovered Montessori, I understood parents' feelings, worries, and hopes very well. Later when I became a teacher I tried my best to share, with parents and grandparents and other family members, information that would help them understand what happens in school, and that would be interesting and helpful at home. Montessori teachers become skilled at observing and meeting the needs of children, but one must also be skilled at observing and meeting the needs of parents. Sometimes it is very difficult for parents to separate from a child at this young age and it is important to understand this and to listen to this parent carefully and reassure them in as many ways possible.

Meetings – Open House with Children

At my school, which was a one-primary-class school in the beginning, we had open houses twice a year just for family and friends of the students. The children brought their parents, and usually sang a song or two for, performing casually for the audience. Having a short performance was a very good way to assure 100% attendance. Parents were alerted ahead of time that singing at the open house was optional, because sometimes a child, who had joined in practicing a song during class, would suddenly develop stage fright in front of an audience. We explained that every child should above all be comfortable and enjoy the evening.

On the day of the open house, which was held just after school or early in the evening, the children prepared during that day by cleaning, and then getting out their favorite work of the day and having it set out when the parents arrived, to show their guests. They sometimes wanted to practice their song during the big day, and occasionally requested that they act out a poem or a finger play. The performance was very short, only 10 minutes or so. Since the open house lasted about 1.5 hours, people arriving and leaving as they pleased, the performance was scheduled for the middle of the evening.

The open house was very casual, completely focused on the happiness of the children, who were individually working with their parents, or sometimes just sitting on the floor with their parents and watching the others. I did not give a talk or make any announcements, unless the children asked me to announce the performance, and there was no food. The parents had been prepared, through the newsletter.

Note: One thing I always stressed in the newsletter in the buildup to the open house, was that any conversation must be between a child and parents, not parents talking with other parents, and not parents talking with me or my assistant.

Meetings Just for Adults

I also had optional parent meetings with slide presentations (which today would be PowerPoints) during which I described and talked about each picture in detail. That was the extent of the presentation. I made sure to have taken pictures of each child, and pictures representing all of the major areas of work. Sometimes the older students were present for this as well, and they sat still with the parents and appeared very mature.

Even though I was sometimes asked to share Montessori philosophy with a small group of interested parents, I found that most parents wanted to see pictures of what was going on in the classroom, to get an idea of what happens, and to find out practical things they could do at home. Pictures of children enjoying dusting, and cleaning furniture, and gardening, and scrubbing the bird bath, and sitting quietly in the library corner reading or looking at a book, and helping each other with their work, gave parents practical ideas.

Lectures

For parents who were interested I invited them to the talks I gave at the local college, for the students in the psychology and sociology classes who had observed in the school. These were especially interesting events because the students had written down their questions while observing our class and they were very interested in getting answers.

One of the reasons I did not give long talks at parent meetings, was that throughout my own traditional schooling years, and into adult life, I have dreaded having to sit still and listen to someone talk, unless it was something I was passionate about, and it was my choice and not required. Almost all of the parents at my school told me that it was much more interesting to see their children's enjoyment of work, either at an open house or by means of pictures.

Newsletter/Books

At that time, most of the books that were written about Montessori education were written by Montessori herself. So, I created a monthly newsletter combining incidences in the class with Montessori philosophy.

Today I share my Montessori work in a blog—stories and experiences in different countries combined with Montessori philosophy—and in books. Always I am thinking about what it was like to be a new Montessori parent and wanting to know more and then being a Montessori teacher and hoping to share just the right amount of information with parents. My books are short, with no secret, exclusive, Montessori language, and with many pictures. What I love hearing are comments like this, "Your books are deep yet so easy to understand. Both my partner and I read them and then we can discuss our children and Montessori together, rather than my being the expert!"

Parent Conferences

In our small community, it was often the case that I was invited to eat a meal with the family of one of my students. I explained ahead of timed that any conversation at these meals should include the child or children, and we would not talk about the child unless it was something brought up by him or her. Parents were very pleased to have this guidance in preparation for our time together. These were always a valuable kind of parent/family conference.

Sometimes a parent, or parents, or grandparents, requested a private meeting with me, or I might suggest one. It is quite normal, when parents were educated in a competitive, graded, system, as I was, to want to know how their child is doing compared to the others.

In the 0-3 Montessori program, we explain to parents that development is basically of movement, of the whole body and the hand, and language. And there is no sense in comparing one's infant to any other because each one has an internal guide directing the development. At one time a child will be working on whole body balance and movement, or the abilities of the hands and fingers, or the development of language. The important thing is to observe and appreciate the work, not to wish the child was working on something one's friend's child is working on.

At the age of the primary class, it is similar, and we follow each child's choice of work. I assured the parents that every child is offered activities from the complete range of possibilities and the choice is the child's. We did not look at the mastery charts! The focus was not on a list of lessons their child had had; instead I shared a few activities that their child really enjoyed, special relationships with others, and little incidences that I might have recorded. But most importantly, together, we looked at their child's concentration graphs. These always showed improvement in concentration over time.

Almost always, after a conference of this kind, parents were more attuned to what the child chose to do at home and how deep and long were the periods of concentration. And at the next conference they were always pleased to share examples.

HUMAN NEEDS
AND TENDENCIES LIST

Transition from Age 0-6 and 6-12

One of the theory lectures that is delivered in any Montessori overview, introduction, or teacher course, is called *Human Needs and Tendencies*. The basic physical needs of humans are food, shelter, transportation, and clothing; but there are other needs, sometimes called *tendencies*, that support human development. Montessori determined that these needs or tendencies exist in each individual, and that they are expressed in unique ways according to the age and stage of development of the person.

When I was a teacher in a Montessori primary class, and later in elementary classes, I kept a list of these needs ready for constant reference. The list helped me whenever I had a question about what to do next with a child. Below are some examples from the list I kept on hand, with a brief explanation of how they are met differently for ages 3-6 and 6-12. There are other needs and tendencies just as important, such as independence, control of error, maximum effort, perfection, self-control, calculation, imitation, abstraction, and creative imagination. Those listed below give some examples of how needs and tendencies change as a child makes the transition to the next level of development.

Exploration

This tendency guides a child to experience the environment with a desire to understand it. We are all explorers in some way: physically, mentally, spiritually, with a desire to learn, to carry out research. For children at age 3-6 we help meet this need by providing a rich, simple, logical environment. This child needs to have the freedom to be able to move about in a safe environment, home, or classroom, or outside in nature. During this absorbent mind period of life much of who a child is comes from what is learned while exploring this environment.

Here is an example of how this need changes in the next stage of development, age 6-12:

> *At this age, there is a gradual transition from motor sensorial exploration to that of the imagination. The child doesn't just want to know that our math system is based on the number 10, but why we have a math system at all, where did it begin, and what use it is to us! This new mind can easily reach back into the past and then reach conclusions about what might be coming in the future. This mind begins to be able to conceive of the tiniest particles of matter as well as the infinity of space. We must not limit them to our own educational experience, but provide ways for these big questions to be researched and answered.*
>
> *Along with exploring the world, now outside the home even more than inside, there will be an exploration in behavior. The child thinks, "How will this new kind of speaking and acting that has been observed on the street be handled if I try it out at home?"*
>
> *— Aid to Life, Montessori Beyond the Classroom*
> *(p 230)*

Order

Order in the home or classroom aids the understanding of one's surroundings, and the classification of new knowledge and impressions. This need is met in a predictable environment, an environment where everything has a certain place. Following the parent or teacher as model, the child delights in learning how to replace items to the proper place. When a child is new to the classroom there will be a period of exploring to discover the order, to find out where everything belongs, the physical order.

There is also a need for a predictable schedule, not by the minute, but one event following another, in a logical and practical order, so the child knows what comes next. This helps to provide security throughout the day.

At age 6-12, order is created more in the mind. The whole of creation is laid before this child, and many projects are inspired. Sometimes the students tend to begin too many projects at once and need adult, or peer, help in organization of plans and work. There is a need for order in time management and planning and completing work. Since there are usually required state or country academic requirements at this age, this child will be developing order in how to meet the required goals, while still having time to follow interests.

Movement

Age 3-6 is the motor-sensorial (movement and senses) period of life. This child does not learn by sitting still and listening to someone talk (unless being told a story or read to from a book by a parent at bedtime of course!) but by moving and interacting with the environment. The best activities are those that require the mind and body to work together for a purpose. There are many examples in the Montessori primary class. There are many activities that help a child master movement of the whole body while walking or carrying things, and in the use of the hands and fingers. This does not mean that the child must be moving in order to be learning! Moving and being still—sitting still or resting or watching others—are determined by the child, not directed by an adult.

At age 6-12, there is the same amount of freedom in movement in class, but at this time the children begin to move and explore outside the classroom, in society. They might be walking more and learning to take public transportation. They still benefit, physically, mentally, and emotionally, from practical life, real work. Sports are valuable at this time because these children are interested in organizing themselves into groups and working together. There is a movement in Montessori today, Montessori Sports, to make sports much less competitive, and in ways where all children get to participate and improve physical skills cooperatively.

Work

Why do we use the word *work* instead of *play*? I think this came about so we adults would realize that the activities found in a Montessori setting are valuable and should not be interrupted. In reality, the activity might be the same, but because it is called *work* the children, and their adults, feel that it is important.

(A real work story) Years ago, a little girl and I were having a conversation about the fact that her family could afford to have a horse, and her friend's family could not. She figured it out. There were four members in her family, the parents working full time and the children in Montessori primary classes. In her friend's family there were three members, the parents working full time and one child in Montessori primary class.

She explained to me, "Our family can afford a horse because all four of us work." It was a delightful insight for me, to see how important she felt her daily work at school was.

At age 6-12 the work continues, gradually less sensorial and more mental, using the imagination. Now the practical life work, caring for the environment, is considered a responsibility to the group. There is no limit to how much academic work the children carry out.

Repetition

I remember seeing a video of a young child doing the Montessori flower-arranging activity for the first time. This little boy had been prepared by learning how to carry objects, to place objects carefully, to pour water, to wipe up spills, etc., all of the direct and indirect preparation for this long and complex task. Now this little boy was ready to put all of these skills together in a great work.

In the video, it was clear that his mind and body was working together for an important task, important not only for his happiness and development, but a social contribution of beautifying the environment.

He put on the flower-arrangement apron (marking the beginning of the cycle of activity). Then he selected a small vase from a collection on a tray on the shelf; then he took a container to the sink for water; then carefully poured water in the vase; then selected a flower from the flower basket and placed it (sometimes more than one) in the vase; then took a little doily from the shelf and placed it on a table; then placed the vase with the flower on the doily. Then he repeated the cycle over and over, until all of the vases with flowers had been placed on the classroom tables. Finally, he took off his apron and hung it up, and then looked, with a satisfied expression on his face, around the classroom, deciding what to do next.

As we learn more and more of the importance of executive function, it is clear that this is a perfect example of the activities necessary to improve these skills. This applied to the child from 6-12 as well as to the adult.

Concentration

I think it has been made clear throughout this book the supreme importance of this need so I am not going to go into detail here. As a teacher, even though I understand the value of not interrupting a child who is experiencing deep concentration on real, challenging work, it was important to have this on my list as a constant reminder.

At a Montessori conference a video was shown that was supposed to explain the difference between a primary and elementary class. In the video almost all, if not all, of the children were moving about and talking. I did not see even one child concentrating. It is important to be aware that, even though this is the age when students want to work together, to talk and carry out projects together, the most important work, the real concentration, occurs when a person is allowed to be quiet and think.

Communication

At age 3-6, children usually prefer to work on something alone, with others nearby focusing on their own work. Visitors are sometimes surprised at the silence of a Montessori primary class when everyone is busy with their own work. But occasionally two or more children will choose to discuss their work with each other and sometimes others join in. And we adults are always there to listen when a child is ready to speak. As models, we try to always give the correct language, with a respectful tone of voice, and to speak to the children with the same respect, in the same tone of voice, we would use with peers.

In the 6-12 class, there is not only more communication among the students, but there are regular study planning meetings, each child communicating privately with the teacher. Students begin to learn how to communicate by giving a presentation to the group. They communicate in a very adult way as they contact, for example, a university lab or a museum, to find out all of the details for planning, and realizing, a research trip. And, just as in the primary class, they learn from the teacher as model to be respectful and polite and considerate, in communicating with anyone.

THE ELEMENTARY
CLASS INTRODUCTION

There are two main differences in observation and recordkeeping in primary classes and elementary classes. First of all, in most places there are state or country requirements that must be taken into consideration in the education of children from age six to twelve. Secondly, because at this age children become more and more capable of planning and executing their own work, the teacher keeps this developing independence and responsibility of the students always in mind.

In my work with Montessori schools in several countries I have seen a great variety in how Montessori philosophy and practice are understood, and how they are carried out in the classroom. In one country for example, every teacher of children in "first grade" was required to be teaching, on a specific day, the same page of the same book, as every other teacher in the country. In this country "Montessori" meant the creation of private classes after school.

I have seen schools with such a mobile expat community that students were seldom part of the Montessori elementary class for more than a year, sometimes less. And I have seen teachers and administrators forced to compromise what could be truly authentic Montessori in order to attract students whose parents might otherwise choose more traditional private schools for their children. But I have also seen schools where Montessori elementary students are getting the very best of authentic Montessori for this age.

My own experience as an elementary teacher followed five years of teaching in Montessori primary classes for children from age two through six. So, I was well aware of the importance of children choosing their own work, and the vital importance of protecting concentration. During those primary years I experimented continually, always following my training and the needs of the children. This experimentation continued when working with elementary students. At this level, the goal was to protect concentration, while meeting the state academic requirements, and allowing the children to spend most of their time forging a unique path of exploration and learning.

I am sharing some of these experiments and systems that were developed during my own elementary classroom teaching years. They have been helpful in schools in many places and I hope they give you some validation of your work, or courage to try new ways.

The main areas of the following chapters are:

The environment

The schedule

State or country requirements

The student/teacher planning meeting

The students' own recordkeeping

The teacher's recordkeeping

Since I have written about this age, from six to twelve in several other books, I will be quoting from these books.

As always, in the end you must base your work, and your experiments in meeting the needs of the child at this age, on careful observation of the students work, success, and happiness.

THE ELEMENTARY CLASS ENVIRONMENT

Inside and Outside Environments

Just as in the primary class, the environment at this level has two parts, inside and outside of the classroom. In the primary class the outside environment is ideally connected to the inside, sometimes with free-flow during the work period, so a child can choose to work in either place.

In the elementary class, there may also be this inside-outside flow, often with activities in gardening and caring for animals. However, at the elementary level, the outside environment includes a larger part of the world beyond the school. It can be exploration in many places in the local community, this elementary activity is called "going out." The students develop the skills to arrange these excursions by themselves, inspired by work that is going on in the classroom.

The Inside Environment, Based on the Five Great Lessons

The five main areas of work in the elementary class are represented in the Five Great Lessons. These are (1) creation of the solar system and the earth, introducing physical sciences (2) evolution of life on earth, introducing the biological sciences (3) arrival and civilizations of humans, introducing studies related to humanity, (4) history and development of human language, and (5) the history and development of math and geometry. The five great lessons are the backbone of cosmic education, the elementary curriculum.

When I am working as a school consultant, and being asked for advice on the environment, one of the first things I look for is how obvious the division of the environment into these five basic areas is to the students. All too often one finds plenty of math and language, but the timelines, charts, science experiment equipment, and all of the other elementary materials are in cupboards, in the teacher's office, or just not available.

In these cases, the first thing I suggest is a rearrangement of the classroom to make all five areas very visible, and everything connected with them—related books, experiment equipment, charts, timelines, and so on—always accessible.

When the classroom is clearly divided into the five basic areas, there is a subconscious constant reminder, a natural sense of balance in academic pursuits, in the mind of the children and the teacher. This creates a firm foundation of the whole idea of cosmic education. Then the two main goals of Montessori elementary education are active: first, the interrelatedness of all parts of reality, and secondly, the breadth of possibilities for discovering one's own special role in life, which we call the *cosmic task*.

The Environment by the Age of the Students

Some classes have the complete age range of six to twelve, but others, perhaps because of state requirements, are divided into two groups of three years, 6-9 and 9-12. If the second division exists then it is important to remember that most of the work—if it is following a child's interest—will be drawn from anywhere in the complete 6-12 range of work no matter how old the child is.

If the age range has been split into 6-9 and 9-12, there are two ways to deal with this: (1) there must be a complete range of 6-12 materials in each class, one set for the 6-9-year-olds, and another complete set for the 9-12-year-olds; (2) if the two classrooms are next to each other there can be a connecting door between the two, always left open, so the children are allowed to collect materials and to work in either area.

Camilla Grazzini, the long-time Montessori 6-12 trainer in Italy, and his wife Baiba remind us, in the AMI "Communications I, 2003" and again in

"Communications 2010 Special Issue," that we must make this decision based on psycho-pedagogical reasons, not the practical, financial, or scheduling reasons of a school. They say that if the children are split into 6-9 and 9-12 classes, that in each class there should be a full set of materials for the full 6-12 age span, so that the children are completely free to work at their own pace in all of the areas of the curriculum. In my experience, I can definitely see the wisdom in this, as it is quite common for a 7-year-old to do 11-year-old work and vice versa. And it would be very rare for a child, without pressure or requirements of the adult, to complete every lesson in every area of the curriculum at the 6-9 level before moving on. There should be instead an atmosphere of peace and steady progress. The teacher's role is to inspire the child to want to do research, to learn more. It is not to require and "teach." As my 6-12 trainer Margaret Stephenson often reminded us, "The teacher is in charge of the minimum, the child the maximum."

— Child of the World, Montessori, Global Education for Age 3-12+, (page 86)

Silence and Noise

All of my life I have been aware of my own need for silence and solitude in order to think clearly, and to work and create. My fondest memories from childhood are not with groups of people, but climbing to the top of a tree, or walking alone along a riverbank, singing. In university or during Montessori teacher training, many students formed study groups, but I had a strong need to prepare, all on my own and in silence. Of course, I am very comfortable with groups and I contribute often to group projects, but my real work is only accomplished when I can concentrate in a space with no distractions.

When I discovered Montessori, where silence is part of the work in the primary class, and respected at all ages, I breathed a sigh of relief. I am very firm, as both a teacher, and now as a consultant, to help others understand the needs, and provide the same respect and opportunity, for people like me.

> *In my own 6-12 classes I have noticed that some children need absolute silence in order to concentrate, while others seem to be unaware of the talking going on around them and are still able to do their individual work, to concentrate deeply. So, in each different place where I taught I arranged, with the help of the children, an area where talking was prohibited and an area where it was allowed. It was interesting to see that the needs of different groups were different, some year the group was made up of mostly those who needed silence, and other years it was the opposite, and so the size of the designated areas also changed. These individual needs must be taken into account in creating an environment where learning can take place.*
>
> *— Child of the World, Montessori, Global Education for Age 3-12+, (page 85)*

Sometimes, when I am at a school for the first time, I observe an extremely noisy and busy elementary Montessori class. In conversation with the teacher I often discover that the teacher had an expectation of such noise, and actually a bit of chaos, that this was the way a Montessori elementary class is "supposed to be." Such an expectation can become a self-fulfilling prophecy.

My own elementary classes were as calm and quiet as the primary, and certainly this was not an imposed quiet, but the situation when each child is deeply involved and concentrating, even if working with a few friends.

This expectation of an elementary class being just as quiet as a primary class was made clear during my elementary training:

> *My teacher trainer, Miss Stephenson, was visiting*
> *an elementary class. It was one of those classes where*
> *children, almost all of the children, are talking all of the*
> *time. After some time, she couldn't take it any longer and*
> *she stood up from the chair where she had been observing*
> *in the middle of the room and called out, "Be quiet!"*
> — *Montessori and Mindfulness, (page 83)*

Practical Life

Sometimes there is the idea that practical life work—care of the person, the environment, and grace and courtesy—is important only during the primary years. After all that is the time when children naturally want to stretch themselves, physically and mentally, to learn all of the tasks they see being carried out in their homes.

Practical life work is very important in the elementary class as well as in the primary. But now this work is approached in a new way, fulfilling the role of a contributing member of a social group.

And all of the cleaning, sorting, organization, anything that concerns care of the environment, should be the responsibility of the children. In preparing the environment at this age I also found that having a book on manners, in the classroom library, was very well received. Even though a lot of it was outdated and even brought forth laughter from the students, it provided a well-needed sense of comfort in knowing about manners of all kinds, and how to show concern and care and respect for others by one's words and actions.

> *In my first 6-12 class after training at this level I had*
> *brought a large, hardcover, etiquette book by Emily Post*
> *into class. This book covered everything from where to*
> *place the silverware and glasses when setting the table, to*

how to address a letter to Royalty. At first it was seen as a curiosity of historical interest, but I noticed, more and more, how much time the older children spent with this book with quite serious expressions on their faces, and how their manners improved.

Later, consulting in an elementary class in Moscow I was asked how to bring more practical life work, real helpful work, into the class at this level. On that day, the classroom assistant was beginning to clean the storage shelves, and two boxes had arrived, each containing a chair that needed to be assembled after class. I suggested that the teacher and assistant take a careful look at everything they themselves do during the day and turn over everything that could be done by a child to the children. The next day a student was organizing the storage shelves much more completely and carefully than an adult might have done, and two students had the metal parts of the new chairs spread out on floor mats and were following the directions to assemble them.

– Montessori and Mindfulness, (page 138)

The Outside Environment, *Going Out*

Going out is as important a factor in arranging the Montessori elementary experience as are books, time lines, charts, experiments, presentations, and anything else. These are not scheduled field trips arranged by adults, but inspiration-based experiences for further exploration inspired by the curiosity of the children, and entirely arranged by them.

These may be shopping for classroom supplies or food, arranging an interview with an expert on a field one or more of the students have become interested in; it can be a trip to satisfy curiosity about the work of wind and water, or different kinds of plants, or an art exhibit that has come to a nearby museum. The examples are endless.

Of course, these trips do not happen in the first week of school because it is important to have the new students develop a level of independence and responsibility in the inside environment first.

A personal example of going out

An example from one of my own classes was inspired by zoology dissections. In studying the internal function of invertebrates and vertebrates, we dissected fish and other ocean creatures bought at the fish market near our class in California. One day as we were dissecting a squid, I shared an experience of watching the octopus hide itself by releasing a cloud of black liquid, which covered the escape. I had seen this in a tank at the Exploratorium in San Francisco. Of course, they wanted to go see this! The Exploratorium, at that time, was a hands-on science museum located in the Palace of Fine Arts, in San Francisco. It was an open-floor plan full of scientific exploration, with offices of scientists carrying our research.

The interest of a few of the students, involved in the initial dissection, resulted in one of the rare, spontaneously-formed all-class meetings. With just a few suggestions from me we started a list of what was necessary in order for all of us, since everyone was interested, to make this trip across the bridge into the city. It involved discussions with families at home, and reports back to the class. A small committee was formed and a notebook begun, and two "scribes" with the best handwriting (decided upon by the group) to be in charge of the notes. This kept track of the progress of gathering information.

Here are some of the items from the list: the address of the museum; who to write to or phone to arrange the visit; how to write a business letter, arranging permission, from the school and each child's parents, for the trip; designing a permission slip to be signed; where to keep the permission slips before and after being signed;

166

figuring out the cost of crossing the Golden Gate Bridge to get into the city; finding out the cost of a ticket to the Exploratorium if there was one; finding out the open hours; finding volunteer parents to drive; figuring out how many cars were needed; how many miles? How much does gas cost per mile? who would pay for the gas; raising money for the trip if necessary; deciding, since it became clear that this would take most of the day, about food for lunch; what did each person need to take along for making notes, drawing pictures; who to write for thanks after the trip, etc. and more . . .

This was one of the first "going out" experiences for this class. We left for San Francisco with a pretty good idea of what was there to be explored beyond the octopus tank, but as long as each small, self-formed group of students stayed together with one of the parent drivers/chaperones, the students could spend the day following their curiosity and their interests, wherever this took them.

When we arrived, and throughout the day, I observed each child, adult, and group, carefully, and took notes for my own observation records. One very outgoing and mature young boy made his way directly to the person who had been the contact for arranging the trip, and introduced himself. One small group had a long discussion, with one of the scientists, of a cow eye dissection exhibit, and arranged to take two eyes back with us to dissect in class. One boy became very interested in Roman architecture because there was an arch-building exhibit, reflecting some of the architecture of the Exploratorium building, that took him back to memories of a similar structure in his primary class. One girl spent half of the day quietly watching, and then drawing, a family of black swans quietly and slowly swimming on the pond just outside the back entrance of the building.

I was surprised that, even though some of these students had lived all of their lives not far from our school which was situated just across the bridge to San Francisco, they had never ever been to the city!

So, now, as part of our classroom environment, we had a notebook in the practical life area of the classroom for planning "going out."

Even if it was just two students arranging to interview a Native American for a civilization project, or two or three "shoppers" interested in finding the best place to buy art supplies for the classroom, or the whole group deciding to visit the Marin County Civic Center that had been designed by Frank Lloyd Wright, the details of each trip were added to the notebook, to be referred to for further excursions.

Going Out Examples

The following is not a list of field trips to be arranged, but just a few examples that might be available not so far from the school. It is helpful for the teacher to have such a list researched, but the inspiration for going out should come from the students and their interests.

Geography: seasonal climatic situations; museums, films, special exhibitions; homes of explorers; lectures given by geographers (appropriate for children); local land and water forms; anything to do with stars, sun, wind, water; a telescope site or planetarium or astronomy museum

Biology: zoos; parks; farms (crops, planting, baby animals); botanical gardens; garden exhibitions

History: interviewing local elders, museums, archaeological sites, and digs; fossil sites; special exhibitions; films (in museums, libraries,), homes of historians; historical homes and buildings; statues; lectures

Cultures: museums and museum exhibits; concerts; opera; art museums; performances; seasonal celebrations; homes of famous artists and musicians

Language and math: typesetting or printing experts; plays; poetry readings, literature or language museum exhibits; publishing houses; bookshops or libraries

THE ELEMENTARY CLASS SCHEDULE
How Much Freedom?

This section is the most difficult for me to write because I have visited so many elementary classes where the teachers' efforts were thwarted, for one reason or another, in their attempts to give freedom—of choice and work and time—to their students.

Children in elementary Montessori classes are introduced to levels of academic studies not usually covered until much later in a traditional school. It is natural for new teachers, in the possession of the incredibly rich teacher albums in the areas of science, history, and so on, to want to give each child the gift of each lesson. But in order to fulfill such a goal, teachers would have to fall back on traditional methods of teaching, or how they themselves were educated in traditional schools: teacher-imposed schedules and assignments, and group lessons. Elementary Montessori teachers need support in their attempts to give students more freedom in time and work—so that they can experience concentration.

> ...to give the whole of modern culture has become an impossibility and so a need arises for a special method, whereby all factors of culture may be introduced to the six-year-old; not in a syllabus to be imposed [. . .] or with exactitude of detail, but in the broadcasting of the maximum number of seeds of interest. These will be held lightly in the mind, but will be capable of later germination, as the will becomes more directive, and thus he may become an individual suited to these expansive times.

> ... the child must learn by [their] own individual activity, being given a mental freedom to take what [they] need, and not to be questioned in [their] choice. Our teaching must only answer the mental needs of the child, never dictate them. Just as a small child cannot be still

because of the need of coordinating movements, so the
older child, who may seem troublesome in his curiosity
over the why, what, and wherefore of everything, is
building up [their] mind by this mental activity, and must
be given a wide field of culture on which to feed.

The task of teaching becomes easy, since we do not
need to choose what we shall teach, but should place all
before him for the satisfaction of his mental appetite. [The
child] must have absolute freedom of choice, and then he
requires nothing but repeated experiences which will
become increasingly marked by interest and serious
attention, during the acquisition of some desired
knowledge.

— Montessori, *To Educate the Human Potential*

Group Lessons

One of the first responses, when I recommend giving more freedom in these areas during a school consultation, is, "But this is the age when students naturally form, and function in groups, so I thought I was supposed to give group lessons."

My reply is that, yes group lessons are very important at times, for example in giving the five great lessons at the beginning of the year, and a few follow-up "key" lessons in each of these areas. But beyond these few examples, group projects are most successful when they are created spontaneously, sometimes instigated by one child, sometimes by several students acting together, sometimes the students requesting the participation and guidance of the teacher.

Here I can again quote Montessori from *To Educate the Hunan Potential*:

. . . interesting fact to be observed in the child of six
is his need to associate with others, not merely for the sake
of company, but in some sort of organized activity. [A

*child] likes to mix with others in a group wherein each has
a different status. A leader is chosen, and is obeyed, and a
strong group is formed. This is a natural tendency,
through which mankind becomes organized.*

The Choice to Work or Not to Work

Sometimes I enter a Montessori elementary class full of noise
and movement. I do not judge, assuming this is a rare situation. But,
upon further observation, in some instances I find that this restless,
unfocused, situation is caused by the fact that there are several
scheduled events or required group lessons each day—and the
students know that any attempt to delve deeply into a project
requiring time and concentration will be interrupted, so they do not
begin.

It is often the case, however, with both children and us adults,
that much important work is being done in the head while the body
appears to be uninvolved with the project at hand.

It is important to give students the opportunity to not be
physically working on anything, but resting and thinking, but this
pause in physical activity should not be because they are avoiding
deep concentration that will be interrupted. Important work can, at
times, occur during a conversation with another person or in a group,
but the highest level of creativity occurs only when one is in solitude.

*There is a lot of evidence to support the value of a
child's contemplation in the classroom. We are mistaken
in thinking that a child must be constantly doing
something with his hands in order to be mindful,
concentrating, or to be using his time in what we would
consider a valuable way. Even the greatest minds learned
that, in creating a great work, no more than a few hours a
day was spent actually "on task" and the rest in
contemplation of the work.*

Here is one example from an article entitled "A Better Way to Work", that explores the work habits of Darwin, Dickens, Ingmar Bergman, and others. (www.nautil.us):

"They only spent a few hours a day doing what we would recognize as their most important work. The rest of the time they were hiking mountains, taking naps, going on walks with friends, or just sitting and thinking. Maybe the key to unlocking the secret of their creativity lies in understanding not just how they labored but how they rested."

— Montessori and Mindfulness (page 41)

Flow – the Essence of Montessori

Some of the reasons that Montessori elementary students learn a lot and often remember what they learn, and can apply this knowledge in many ways, are these: they have chosen the work; they enjoyed the work; concentration on the work was respected and not interrupted; the work made them happy, and kind. The study of work as happiness is best expressed in the idea of *flow*.

Mihály Csikszentmihalyi, Hungarian psychologist, is noted for his study of what makes life worth living, in **happiness** *and* **creativity**. *He is best known for his research on what he calls* **flow** *which can be described as deep concentration on an activity not because someone has told one to do it, or for any kind of reward or praise, but for its own sake, intrinsically motivated. During the experience of flow, time flies, and every action, movement, and thought follows inevitably from the previous one. One's whole being is involved, and one is using one's skills to the utmost. Dr. Csikszentmihalyi's research has shown that people are happiest when they are in the state* *of flow. And this occurs when they are working on something. How did he discover this?*

He developed the Experience Sampling Method at the University of Chicago in the early 1970s. Each person participating in the study wore a pager that was programmed to "beep" at random times during the day. When this happened the activity and what the subject was thinking about and where he was were all recorded. This has provided valuable insight into the questions of what makes a person happy. For example, he discovered that such simple activities of gardening, cooking, making music, and even working are very likely to be experienced as flow, but passive leisure activities such as watching television or relaxing are not. At least 10,000 people from all over the world have now participated in these studies of flow.

—*Montessori and Mindfulness* (page 51)

Here is an example of an experiment with high school students in China. Each student was given a pager programmed to go off at 10 unpredictable times during a school day. Each time the pager sounded, the students were instructed to identify what they were doing, what they were thinking about, and how they are feeling.

The teacher was giving a very interesting and entertaining whole-group lesson on the Genghis Khan. As the students' pagers went off during the lesson this is what the students recorded as their thoughts:

"Of 27 students in the class, 25 didn't mention anything vaguely connected with China; they mentioned their dates, their coming football game, how hungry they were, how sleepy they were, etc. There were 2 who mentioned China but nothing about the Genghis Khan."

174

– *"Flow and Education"*, *The NAMTA Journal Vol. 22, no. 2, 1997*
  – *Montessori and Mindfulness* (page 53)

Concentration is Still the Primary Goal

If you look back on the chapters in the primary class section of this book, you can see the information on Montessori's concentration graphs, or work curves. This concept is important in working with children and young adults at any age. When I was teaching elementary classes, even though I did not track concentration with these concentration graphs, watching for improvement in the level of concentration of each student was always on my mind.

Elementary students have the potential for far longer periods of concentration if given support. Although the primary class concentration graph tracked a period of three hours of a morning (and sometimes three hours in the afternoon as well), the length of concentration at the elementary class level can be days or weeks. As Montessori says in *The Advanced Montessori Method, Vol. I*:

> *The elementary school period presents itself . . . as a continuation of the 'Children's Houses' . . .. We see a child occupied for seven or eight consecutive days with the same work. Another child becomes interested in the potentialities of the arithmetical frame, and perseveres with the same work for days, until his knowledge of it has matured.*

At this age, age six to twelve, children can be given the chance, the tools, and the trust, of being completely in charge of the whole school day, week, year. That is the way these students will be able to create themselves anew, to go to the limits of curiosity and interests, to satisfy the creative impulse, and to become responsible members of society.

As I said in the beginning of this book, education with a daily, weekly, yearly schedule of subject, assignments, and goals, already decided by adults, is nothing I would have been interested in participating in.

It is so exciting to begin a school year with a group of children at this age when the teacher has no clue as to what subjects will eventually have been covered, where curiosity and passion will have taken the group, and how and where community beyond the classroom will have been tapped for information. Even though at this age there are required academic goals, when the students are given the tools and the experience to manage their time, and work, and responsibility, the Montessori elementary class can be relaxed, successful, creative, and enjoyable for all.

THE ELEMENTARY CLASS
STATE/COUNTRY REQUIREMENTS

Born originals,
how comes it to pass that we die copies?
— Edward Young, 18th Century British Philosopher Poet

Help Meeting the Basics

A child at this age wants to explore in sometimes unexpected directions, to follow interests and to create, individually and with friends. This can only occur when the school day is free from study requirements and time limits.

During my elementary teacher training I learned that Montessori herself suggested that we make available to the children the traditional school curriculum for their age range: the subjects that would be covered in the traditional school clearly listed by grade. Referring to this brief overview provides a feeling of security for both the students and their families as students make their own unique work plans.

In my elementary classes I made a one-page outline of the state requirements for each grade level, and hung them on the wall for easy reference by the children. If you have a class of children who will be with you for many years these lists could show just the general expectations for grades one to three, and another list for grades three to six, so they are not tied to annual expectations. We should be clear that this is a very brief list for each grade or three-year span!

Today, just as with Montessori schools, there is a growing number of private and public alternative schools. One example is the Waldorf school system that is based on the ideas of Rudolf Steiner, 20th Century philosopher and social reformer. As a contrast to the list above, here is a list of requirements for second grade in a typical Waldorf school:

> English: *fables from around the world, the study of the saints, introduction to reading, grammar*
>
> Mathematics: *continuing work with the four processes (simple addition, subtraction, multiplication, and division), column algorithms (an example would be the math problem 24+24=48, presented in a vertical column)*
>
> Form Drawing: *running forms (drawing patterns, repeated in horizontal rows), leading to cursive handwriting*
>
> Nature Study: *Aesop's fables, work of Thornton W. Burgess, Native American stories*
>
> Music: *Singing and Recorder*
>
> Handwork: *Knitting, Crochet*
>
> Eurhythmy: *(body movement accompanied by live instrumental music or by the human voice in spoken poetry and tales)*
>
> Foreign Language: *in songs and greetings*
>
> Painting and Modelling (clay)

As an elementary teacher, I found that this work related to a grade level in a traditional education system took my students an average of no more than two hours a week. In this way, the children can focus on all of the doors opened in the elementary Montessori Cosmic Education work, often work that an adult would never require and predict!

Observing the Students' Progress

As long as the required work is being done, and the students are focused and concentrating—working or thinking—during the day, there is no need to know exactly what each student is doing at every moment. In the next chapters, there will be more details on helping the students, and the teacher, keep track of the work.

This story helped me keep this in mind. It was told during our elementary training by Margaret Stephenson. At the time, she was the teacher in an elementary class England. A government education official was visiting the class to see "what this Montessori way of learning was all about". The official noticed a child way off by himself, quietly working in a far corner of the room.

"What is he doing?" she asked Miss Stephenson.

"I have no idea. Shall we go find out?" was her slightly humorous but proud reply.

It was clear to me that Miss Stephenson trusted the children to be always doing something valuable, her point being to us was that it is not necessary, often not helpful, for the teacher to micromanage children.

Tests

In our own state of California there is a standard test at the end of grade six in all public schools that is also available to private schools and homeschoolers. In Montessori classes the students have a few timed practice tests to prepare them for this event. For many, this is the very first experience in scores, time limits of work, grades, and competition. Here is an interesting story:

> *Many of Michael's friends attended public school*
> *and he often heard them worrying about an upcoming*
> *test, something outside of his educational experience until,*
> *in a class on music theory at the Saturday Music*
> *Academy, he was given a test.*
> *That evening as we were having dinner he said:*
> *"I don't see what the big deal is about tests. My*
> *friends who go to school are always worrying about them.*
> *The music test today was no problem. If I didn't know the*

answer to a question I just looked at the test of the person sitting next to me."

We had to laugh and were able to explain the concept of "cheating." Michael was used to working with, not competing against, others to solve problems. This was his first experience of being asked to give information completely on his own, where his answers would be marked right or wrong by someone else, and then he might be given a grade compared to the grades earned by the other students in the class.

We explained that a test could be seen as a way to find out if a teacher was successfully imparting knowledge, and to assess the progress of a student and then give direction where he should focus his energy and time in order to improve. We explained the traditional testing situation in a positive way, but it gave us a lot to think about.

But actually, we didn't pay much attention to these requirements because Michael was thriving and happy with the way we were homeschooling and he was learning all the time not just during what would have been "school" hours.

As Ted Dintersmith, PhD, says in his book What School Could Be (Princeton University Press, 2018):

"Bulk tests don't lend themselves to higher-order competencies like creativity, communication, critical analysis, collaboration, leadership, tenacity, and entrepreneurship."

"Across America our kids study what's easy to test, not what's important to learn. It's easy to test factual content and low-level procedures, so that defines the curriculum."

— Montessori Homeschooling, One Family's Story
(page 104)

It was standard in our local homeschooling community, and the students agreed, to take the public-school tests at the end of sixth grade, or elementary school. This was because some of the students would stop their homeschooling at that point and begin traditional middle school. The tests were carried out by traditional public-school teachers. In our family, we paid very little attention to the traditional public-school requirements. Instead we focused on answering questions and following curiosity. Below are the results of that test. You can imagine that we were a bit apprehensive, but the results gave our family the courage to continue with our unique Montessori path of education.

> *At the end of sixth grade, age twelve, this
> Montessori homeschooler took the Woodcock-Johnson
> Tests of Achievement given to students in many schools.
> Here is a rough sketch of the results by grade equivalency.
> A score 6.9 is the average for the end of sixth grade; a
> score of 12.9 is the average for the end of the senior year of
> high school:*
>
> *Language: Word comprehension: 16.8; Passage
> comprehension: 15.6*
>
> *Math; Calculation: 7.3; Applied problems: 10.8*
>
> *Science: 10.4*
>
> *Social Studies: 13.1*
>
> *Humanities: 14.6*
>
> *— Montessori Homeschooling, One Family's Story*

(page 177)

Education as Preparation for Life

This sentence is repeated throughout all of the Montessori work, for any age. But at the end of the elementary years, as students leave the last of childhood, and become young adults, it is especially important to keep it in mind.

It was my first year teaching an elementary class, a group of children from six through thirteen years of age. One member of the class, who had just joined us, had been in "free schools" in California throughout his elementary years. He had not been required to learn much, certainly not the basic requirements for the state of California. I well remember his struggle trying to learn the multiplications tables, how to construct a proper sentence with a capital letter at the beginning and a period or question mark at the end, at age thirteen. One day, frustrated as he attempted to test himself on memorization of the tables, he threw his pencil across the room and burst into tears. It was clear that he needed a uniquely creative approach, and as he was entering the early adult stage of life, something more practical. Here is a quote from another book that tells more.

> A very bright 13-year-old boy was having trouble concentrating on math and other purely intellectual subjects, so I watched carefully to discover his real abilities and interests, which were: house, job, music, and parenting. In our class, the children designed and developed long-term research projects and presentations. This boy was behind in academic areas so I helped him weave his interests into projects that would utilize skills that he needed to practice.

> He spent hours planning his dream house, complete with an indoor swimming pool and skateboard area. In doing this he researched houses of various cultures and used plenty of math, graphing, and geometry in constructing the house plans.

> He did a feasibility study for beginning a skateboard construction-and-repair business–rents, prices of

equipment, market value of skateboards and labor costs.
As his confidence grew he branched out into other
academic areas. Then he became interested in literature,
and began to study piano, recorder, and guitar in class
using classical and folk instruction books and asking for
help when he needed it. This study of music provided the
greatest practice in self-discipline as he scheduled daily
practice and was still able to complete his other work. It
seemed to help him express the changing emotions that
otherwise would have no constructive outlet. And the
personal and social rewards were immediate.

But along with this classroom success it was this
boy's interest in parenting that was most intriguing to
observe. Here was this tall, gangly, adolescent boy,
leading the group on the softball field, but if he heard a cry
or yell of one of the children in the 3-6 class at the other
end of the campus, he immediately put down the bat and
ran to see what was the matter. There was one three-year-
old in particular, Paloma, who seemed to have captured
his fathering heart. They had only just met at the
Montessori school, but he could single out her voice from
all others, from quite a distance, and would always go to
her aid. More than anything else, at this time when
intellectual skills had been low it was his being needed as a
protector by the young that gave him a feeling of worth.
– Child of the World; Montessori, Global Education
for Age 3-12+ (page 129)

Over the years I have had many experiences that made me
question the goals of what is considered a standard education.
For example, in 1971, when I was studying in England, a news
report said that such a high percentage of students were aiming
for "A levels" of school work in order to prepare for

university, that there were now too many university graduates for the number of available jobs, and, at the same time, there was a great need for skilled people in other areas. Today, in many places, it is still thought that going to university is the most important goal in life, even though there could be a better goal, a better match for an individual, that would be more valuable for that person and also society.

One winter, when all of the pipes froze at our first home after moving here to the rural area of Northern California, the man who came to remedy the situation was also a professor of history at the local university. He loved figuring out what was wrong, how to solve mechanical problems, and working outside. He told us that he earned much more money, and had more fun, as an emergency home repair person than a university professor and was going to switch professions.

Later, when we were building our present home, the plumber was from South Africa, and he actually had a degree in plumbing, earned in his home country. He told us that when he came to this country he was shocked to find that anyone could hang out a sign that announced "plumber," with no training or expertise whatsoever. We clearly need to support a variety of our students' interests in preparing for life.

> *An ideal culture is one that makes a place for every human gift.* —Margaret Mead, 20th Century American cultural anthropologist

> *Education should not limit itself to seeking new methods for a mostly arid transmission of knowledge: its aim must be to give the necessary aid to human development. This world, marvelous in its power, needs a 'new man'. It is therefore the life of man and his values that must be considered. If 'the formation of man' becomes*

the basis of education, then the coordination of all schools from infancy to maturity, from nursery to university, arises as a first necessity.

— Montessori, *From Childhood to Adolescence*

THE ELEMENTARY CLASS STUDENT/TEACHER PLANNING MEETING

At this age, an education should focus on concentration, increasing independence, following one's curiosity, and the development of responsibility, as well as academics. But it is also the teacher's responsibility to also make sure that the basic state or country requirements discussed in the last chapter are also covered.

Beyond this required work—as long as students are not interfering with the work of others—students should be free of any intrusion, any limits that interfere with their individual pursuits that are the result of a growing curiosity about the world and about life. Such interests usually begin with the five great lessons of cosmic education.

We want to help the development of skills such as being responsible for work for the whole day, then the whole week, and longer. This includes planning and experiments in time management as the students may have ideas different than ours on how to plan and execute research and work. Freedom and support in practicing these skills helps students discover themselves, their learning styles, their individual mental and physical and social needs, their individual inborn gifts, and unique creativity. What an excellent preparation for a responsible and satisfying adult life.

How do we help the student to meet responsibilities, to explore in all directions, and to keep a balance in academic and social life? One method is the individual student/teacher planning meetings.

First Year Students – Weekly Meetings

Individual weekly planning meetings with the teacher are essential for first year students. In these meetings, the pair go over what has been accomplished since the last meeting. Together the student and teacher make a suggested plan for the following week. In some of my own classes students posted their plans on a bulletin board, in other classes they kept them on an individual clipboard, with other work in progress.

Even though I often suggested a certain area of work, I always respected a student's desire to try different time-management schedules. For example, one student might want to do everything on the list in the beginning of the week and check them off and then explore new areas. Another might decide to try tackling something from the list each morning. It is an extremely valuable preparation for life to already be experimenting with time management at this age.

Sometimes, when necessary, the student and I would take a look at the state/country requirements for that "school grade." If the requirement had something to do with grammar or math, for example, we would discuss the various materials in the classroom that would contribute to that necessary accomplishment. It is important for students to understand that meeting these requirements is essential, and being responsible for them allows freedom to explore to one's heart's content.

Older Students – Meeting Less Often

Some second-year students still require a weekly meeting while others, whose work habits have become ingrained, may only need a meeting every two weeks. If a student has developed intensive work habits and interests, it may only be necessary to have this meeting even less often. The students get the idea that they need our help only at the stage of developing work habits, but they will still sometimes come to the teacher and ask for a meeting to make plans, even when we might think a planning meeting is not necessary.

In the next chapter, you will read about a system that I developed that helped with the progress of students developing work habits, time management, and responsibility for meeting the required standards, and keeping a balanced experience throughout all of the five areas of the elementary cosmic education curriculum.

Great Work, Initiated by Students

Even though there is a plan for the week, it is a suggested plan. It is always set aside when student's imagination, curiosity, and independent thinking initiate a project, sometimes called a great work, that would never be required by an adult. These great works are common in the elementary class.

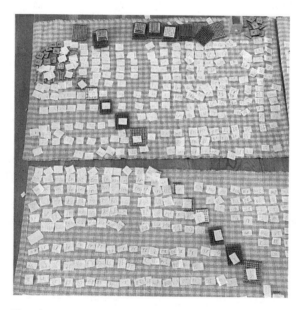

Here is one example: "Squaring the Alphabet"

Two girls in an AMI school in England, having learned about geometry, algebra, and math with sensorial materials in the primary such as the cube of the binomial, the cube of the trinomial and the decanomial, have set a task for themselves that took them two full days. They decided to square the alphabet. So instead of having a+b or a+b+c, or the ten letters of the decanomial, they will have

*26 letters forming the giant square -- a+b+c+d+e+f+g . . .
and so on.*

— Montessori and Mindfulness (page 120)

The follow-up work of the five great lessons lasts
throughout the child's years in the class. The discoveries
related to each great lesson develop parallel to each other,
the students moving back and forth from history, biology,
music, language, geometry, and all of the areas of study,
and they discover that all learning is ultimately related.
Each year the children, as they grow older, delve deeper
and deeper into the many lessons of the basic curriculum,
sometimes going places that none of us expected, and so
teaching us adults, to also appreciate knowledge in a new
way.

What good is knowledge if it is not combined with
consideration for others? Peace is not studied as an
independent subject, but with the study of examples from
the past, and practice in serving food, caring for, and
helping each other. Peace is the natural outcome of a
method of education where children experience work with
their hands and minds working together, for long periods
of individual concentration and contemplation. In this
way, they are able to process and recover from all the
input of our modern world. They learn that peace is not
just the absence of war, but it is the way we feel inside, in
the way we treat each other in our daily lives, the way we
communicate, and the way we solve problems. Children
learn from experience, that peace begins inside a person, at
home, at school. Quoting Montessori:

"The acts of courtesy which [the student] has been
taught with a view to making contacts with others must
now be brought to a new level. The question of aid to the

*weak, to the aged, to the sick, for example, now arises. If,
up to the present, it was important not to bump someone
in passing, it is now considered more important not to
offend that person. While the younger child seeks
comforts, the older child is now eager to encounter
challenges. But these challenges must have an aim. The
passage to the second level of education (age 6-12) is the
passage from the sensorial, material level to the abstract.
A turning toward the intellectual and moral sides of life
occurs at the age of seven."*

    — *Child of the World; Montessori, Global Education
for Age 3-12+* (page 89)

Conclusion

As the teacher and student gather periodically for planning
meetings, there is often a tendency to focus only on the academics.
This quote by Einstein is in agreement with one of the main goals in
Montessori, to prepare students to thrive in a completely
unpredictable future.

    *It is not enough to teach a specialty. Through it one
may become a kind of useful machine but not a
harmoniously developed personality. It is essential that
the student acquire an understanding of and a lively
feeling for values. He must acquire a vivid sense of the
beautiful and the morally good. Otherwise he — with his
specialized knowledge — more closely resembles a well-
trained dog than a harmoniously developed person. He
must learn to understand the motives of human beings,
their illusions, and their sufferings in order to acquire a
proper relationship to individual fellow men and to the
community.*

These precious things are conveyed to the younger generation through personal contact with those who teach, not — or at least not in the main — through textbooks. It is this that primarily constitutes and preserves culture. This is what I have in mind when I recommend the 'humanities' as important, not just dry specialized knowledge in the fields of history and philosophy.

Overemphasis on the competitive system and premature specialization on the ground of immediate usefulness kill the spirit on which all cultural life depends, specialized knowledge included. It is also vital to a valuable education that independent critical thinking be developed in the young human beings, a development that is greatly jeopardized by overburdening him with too much and with too varied subjects (point system). Overburdening necessarily leads to superficiality. Teaching should be such that what is offered is perceived as a valuable gift and not as a hard duty. — Albert Einstein, "Education for Independent Thought," (New York Times, 1952

— Child of the World; Montessori, Global Education for Age 3-12+ (page 89)

TEACHER'S WORK
AND RECORDKEEPING

First of all, the teacher must keep track of the students' meeting of the basic state/country education requirements for the six years of elementary school. Secondly the teacher must open the door for each area of Montessori elementary curriculum, the five great lessons that are designed to awaken a child's imagination and curiosity. Just as at any age, periods of deep concentration on appropriate work, that has been chosen by the individual, is the path to physical, mental, and emotional balance. The observation and recordkeeping of this balance will be intimately connected with the work accomplished.

Beginning with the Great Lessons

The first great lesson—the creation of the universe, the solar system, and earth—is given on the first day of the year. As with each of the great lessons, it lays the foundation for many further discoveries. In the case of the first lesson, for example, this includes astronomy, the solar system, stars, galaxies, comets, constellations, meteorology, chemistry, physics, geology, and physical geography.

Every student, from age six to twelve, is invited, new students are required to attend. In my experience, it is such a welcomed celebration of the beginning of each new year that all students, from age six to twelve, always come to these lessons. If your school divides the elementary level into 6-9 and 9-12, the great lessons should be given in both classes each year. All of the educational materials must be present in both classes and there is no way to predict at what point a child will develop an interest in one of the areas.

Within the first two weeks, all five great lessons are given and this provides an introduction to the whole cosmic education curriculum. Through a variety of tools and experiences, the students will become aware of interrelationships—the universe, plants and animals, humans and the tools of language and math. They will begin to think about the fact that each of us has the potential to play an important role in this reality.

Wisdom from a Master Teacher

I will share some of a recent conversation with John McNamara, a good friend of mine who has been a Montessori elementary teacher for many years, and who is now a consultant and speaker, inspiring other teachers:

> *The only lessons that I give to the whole class are the Great Lessons. Less is more when it comes to lessons. I don't know how many times a student has gotten upset at me when I attempted to interrupt the student in order to give a lesson. I am still learning.*
>
> *I really believe that over-emphasis on curriculum causes the stress and causes the teachers to ask themselves the question, "How can I get the students to do what I want?" (cover the curriculum) instead of more important questions. For example,*
>
> *-What do my students need?*
>
> *-How can I meet these needs?*
>
> *-Under what conditions are students most likely to feel that they can be successful?*
>
> *-When are students most likely to become curious?*
>
> *Teachers have to observe their students more and observe when they are truly engaged because, **A busy student is not necessarily an engaged student.***

John shared one of his favorite Montessori quotes from *The Secret of Childhood*:

> *When because of favorable circumstances work flows naturally from an inner impulse, it assumes an entirely*

193

different character, even in adults. When this happens, work becomes fascinating and irresistible and raises a man above his diverted self. Examples of this may be found in the toils of an inventor, the discoveries of explorers, and the paintings of artists.

Supporting Concentration and Independence

How can a teacher be sure that the basic state/country requirements are met, inspire the students to explore and work hard, offer the essential "key" lessons that follow the great lessons, and avoid group lessons? That is the challenge.

I will share the solution I came up with, not out of my own head, but working together with the students, listening to their problems and solutions. If you look back to the chapter in the primary class section, "Mastery Charts", you will see that there is a chart for every area of the primary curriculum. Each chart has the names of the activities or lessons within that area, and the name of each student. The teacher marks in a box when a lesson has been given, and again when that work has been mastered by the student.

So, I thought to myself, "Why not do the same thing at the elementary class but put the students in charge?" and that is what happened.

On the next page is part of the mastery chart for the elementary class grammar boxes. I created a "mastery chart" for each area, each of the botany and physics experiments, each impressionistic chart, each step of the math curriculum, a chart for the state/country requirements, and so forth. Each mastery chart was fastened to a clip board, a pencil attached by a string, and placed in the appropriate area of the classroom. The children themselves were in charge of recording. They marked a vertical line in the box when they had received a lesson, and crossed the line, making an "X" when they had mastered it.

When I first made the mastery charts I thought about just listing the key lessons, but in discussing it with the students it was clear that they wanted to have everything listed so they could keep track of their progress.

LANGUAGE	child's name	child's name	child's name	child's name	child's name	child's name	child's name	child's name	child's name	child's name	child's name	child's name	child's name	child's name	
Grammar 1															
Grammar 2															
Grammar 3															
Grammar 4															
etc.															

Surprising Results

The independence of the students immediately improved tenfold. When a student was looking for something new to explore the place to look was on one of the clipboards.

When a student and I were having our weekly planning meeting, and a student expressed an interest in something that another student had been seen enjoying, we went right to that area and checked the list.

But most surprising was, when a student wanted to have the next lesson in a subject, rather than coming to me, the student often just went to one of the clipboards to see which fellow student had an "X" in the box related to that work!

Then, being careful not to interrupt if that person was concentrating, asked for a lesson.

From that point on I could not believe how much time I had now to work on materials, make myself a cup of tea, have a casual conversation with a student, observe levels of concentration, keep other kinds of records, and even to practice the piano or the guitar!

195

Key Lessons and Mastery Charts

I have heard it said that in order to assure that children at this age learn to work together one must give most of the lessons to groups. I have never found this to be true. It is impossible to prevent groups forming as it is the natural way of being at this age! Very few group lessons are required after the first two weeks. Those that are given are called *key lessons*. It is only necessary for a student to receive one "key" lesson as follow-up, in each main area of the five great lessons, not all of the possible lessons that follow.

Here are some examples.

The first one is in the area of Botany. The second great lesson, the coming of life on earth, introduces the evolution of plants and animals through the eras. One area of follow-up work includes plant experiments.

One of the key lessons here would introduce the "command cards" for botany experiments. Each card contains the name of the experiment, the materials to be gathered, each step of the activity, and the conclusion.

After the key lesson on the use of the command card, the student can work on without help.

The second example is in the language area. After the fourth great lesson that tells the story of the development of language throughout history there are several "key" lessons.

One key lesson that each student needs is on the use of the grammar boxes. There are several boxes for each part of speech. The boxes are empty and the accompanying filler boxes contain little cards for the work.

There are many steps: oral introduction, the child filling the box with the little cards, reading and acting out the commands on the slips, putting the cards in order, mixing them up and reading them, working with a friend to see how silly the sentence is when not in the correct order, and there will be heard lots of laughter at times.

This work can lead to curiosity about how the use of different parts of speech might have come into being long ago, the etymology of words, and so much more. After this introduction, the key lesson with the first grammar box, the child can work on independently.

A Grammar Box Story

If you look at the grammar box chart above you will see numbered "grammar 1, grammar 2, etc.," referring to each of the grammar boxes. One day, a new student, ten years old and completely new to Montessori, was given the key lesson on the grammar boxes. Rather than going through all of the possible steps and activities listed above, he did the bare minimum. He took in turn each grammar box to a table, filled the empty grammar box with the appropriate cards from the filler box, read the phrase or sentence, put the cards back in the filler box, returned the grammar box to the shelf and moved on. No experimenting, no transposition of the order of words, no laughter. His goal clearly was to fill in as many boxes on the grammar box mastery chart, as quickly as possible. At the end of the day he brought the mastery chart to me to show his work. As he handed me the chart showing all of the boxes he had filled in he looked around the class, perhaps hoping for the other students to witness the high praise of the teacher. I smiled and said something like, "My goodness you have been busy! Did you enjoy this work"?

This was not what he was expecting. He had been operating on his previous experience in schools, get the work done and please the teacher. He returned to the work the next day, starting over, and this time worked with friends, and had fun, and probably a much better chance of learning and remembering grammar.

The First AMI Primary Course in Thailand

I would like to share an experience I had some years later. I was in charge of one of the practicals, or practice, rooms for the first primary course in Thailand. In this space students becoming Montessori teachers were to practice giving lessons to each other. The students of a teacher trainer course, as some readers will know, can be almost overwhelmed by keeping track of lecture notes, practicing with materials, and making their albums.

As was suggested in my own primary training, I urged them to study their notes describing a specific presentation or lesson the lecturer had given; leave the lecture notes out of the practicals room; practice giving the lesson to another adult; make corrections based on what they learned trying to give these lessons; and only then write up the lecture for their albums. It was necessary to practice some of these lessons more than others and sometimes difficult to keep track. It was also very helpful to give practice lessons to as many adults as possible in order to experience the variety of reactions to a lesson.

So, I created "mastery charts" like the one I had used in my elementary classes. The teachers in training put tiny checks in the box each time they practiced a lesson. This helped ensure each student that they had practiced each lesson, and in some cases, how many times. Just as I had seen in elementary classes, a student could look at the mastery chart to see who had practiced a particular lesson, and ask that person for a lesson.

Teacher's Backup and Other Records

It is necessary to periodically make copies, or in some other way, keep a back-up copy of all of the work recorded, just in case something happens to the clipboard.

I know that many people reading this are thinking of how to do this on a computer, and I look forward to what systems can be created, avoiding as much as possible screens, and giving the students more and more responsibility and independence.

In the primary part of this book, there are many suggestions for observation and recordkeeping. Many of these will be helpful in tracking the social, mental, physical, and emotional development of the child in the elementary years.

STUDENTS' WORK
AND RECORDKEEPING

One of the most enjoyable aspects of being a Montessori teacher is that the teacher continues to learn from the students. So, I would put at the top of a list of student work *teaching the teacher*. In the previous chapters, we explored the state/country requirements for the elementary class, the student/teacher planning meeting, and the teacher's work. Most of the information on the students own work has been covered, but there are a few more elements to think about. Here are some stories, examples of what my students taught me.

Story 1: Does Freedom of Schedule Work?

It was my first year of teaching. This was a class of children mostly new to Montessori, from ages six to thirteen years. I had explained the basic requirements, given the first and second great lessons, and all students had their suggested list of work for the following week. I had assured them that as long as they completed their list in the agreed upon time, they were free to decide when to do the work, free to explore the library and read, free to sit and think; the only restriction was that they were not free to interrupt another person who was concentrating without that person's permission.

A few of the students were already very good at reading and I had gone through the rather large school library, that opened directly onto our classroom, and made sure that all of the books—classic literature, historical novels, non-fiction of all kinds—were appropriate. The following morning, we began the new system.

Day one: Everyone was occupied and happy, two or three of the older students were only exploring the library, then lying on the rug in the classroom, or sitting at a table, and reading.

Day two: The students who had done nothing but read the previous day continued to read.

Day three, morning: Reading. I struggled in my mind, "Does this kind of freedom really work? Should I intervene? Should I remind them of their lists even though I said I would not? Are they going to turn out to be completely unprepared for future tests? And so on.

But then my mind went back to a story Hilla Patell had shared with us during our 3-6 diploma course. She had almost interrupted a little girl who was looking around the room, not paying any attention to the geometric solid materials on the floor mat in front of her. The story of how interrupting the girl, rather than observing and waiting, might have prevented the discovery of the three-dimensional geometric shape of the classroom. So, with this memory in mind, I waited.

After the third day's lunch, the students went back to work, the readers put their books away, looked at their lists, and got to work.

Story 2: Rewards and Gold Stars vs Bowling

Sometime in the first weeks of my first year I was approached by a few of the students with a complaint. Most of them had been, until now, in more traditional schools. I was told quite clearly that they were having trouble getting their work finished because they were used to working for grades or some kind of reward. We called a class meeting and had a fascinating discussion on the subject. It was suggested that everyone who completed their work by lunch time on Friday would get to go bowling during the afternoon. A vote was taken and everyone agreed.

Beginning on Monday morning it was like a hive of bees. But by Friday lunch time there were still a few students who had not completed their agreed-upon work. They stayed behind with the school cook as the rest of the students and I went bowling. It was not at all as fun as anyone had expected, definitely not a reward because everyone was feeling bad for the students who were left at the school, even though most of the students had never met the others before, and this was early in the school year. The bowling plan ended early and we returned to school to have another meeting.

At the second whole-class, there was another fascinating discussion. The new plan stated that if EVERYONE finished their work by Friday lunch they ALL would go bowling together.

The following week was a dream, the students were devoted not only to completing their work, but checking in with the other students' lists (in this class all of the lists were posted together on a bulletin board) and offering to help the students who were slow in finishing. This was one of the most beautiful experiences of my teaching career. On Friday afternoon we all went bowling,

But what was even more satisfying, was the feeling of support all of the students had for each other. An all-class group had formed and they felt responsible for each other. They had learned the age-old adage that happiness can come from helping others. Bowling was never mentioned again.

Story 3: No Need for a Teacher

It was by this time well into the fall semester that same year. The school, and our living quarters, were in an old sugar plantation building in the middle of the Caribbean Island of St. Croix. I had become sick with an infection in my throat and could not get up one morning. The head of school assigned the assistant from one of the primary classes to be the adult in my elementary class.

By midmorning my sleep was interrupted by a delegation of three students of our class. They were insulted, indignant. Their report went something like this, "This woman is treating us like children. We know what to do. We don't need a babysitter!"

I asked them to speak to the head of school. The students explained that they had their lists and did not need any help in getting on with their work. So, it was agreed, no adult would actually be in the classroom, even though there were adults on the campus if needed. No adult was needed in the next three days as I gradually got well.

Journals

In my elementary classes, each child had two traditional school "composition" books. One with lines, one with squares. The journal with squares was used for math, algebra, geometry. The journals with lines were used for language, and all other subjects. Each child also had a folder for special drawings, etc. These journals were used only on special occasions to record something very special; they were not a daily requirement! There was no need to keep track of everything done because this record was easily accessible on the student-recorded mastery charts.

The journals were beautiful creations for when a student wanted to remember a poem, a math work, a botany, or physics experiment, sometimes even a small version of one of the impressionistic charts. The journal selections were recorded very carefully, with the best handwriting, sometimes in colored pencils, and often the students decorated the margins. Each page was a piece of art.

One year, in a different elementary class, this time in California, there was a television special of the astrophysicist Carl Sagan called "Cosmos." One of the students saw it at home and gave an enthusiastic report the next day. It was very much in line with what we were talking about after the first great lesson, the creation of the universe and the earth. From then on, the students who were able to, watched the episodes at home and shared the information the next day to those who didn't have a television.

Here is a page from one of the beautiful pages of a student's journal. In case the words are not clear, and I don't even know if they were original with the student but they were beautifully recorded in a journal:

Twinkle twinkle little star

I know exactly what you are.
Up above the world so high,
Like a diamond in the sky.
If you wonder how I know,
Carl Sagan told me so.

Beautiful Journals as Family Keepsakes

A few years ago, our granddaughter, who was at this time in a Montessori elementary class looked through the beautiful journals that her mother had created during her own time in a Montessori 6-12 class. Each page, the subject chosen by her mother—probably no more than one page done every few weeks—was a work of art. The text was illustrated and sometimes the margins decorated, both executed in colored pencils. She spent a lot of time, looking at each page very carefully. Then she came to me and said, "What does the word 'priceless' mean?"

I replied, "It means something is so precious that no amount of money could purchase it."

Her reply? "These journals are priceless."

Daily Work Record, with Time Recorded,
as a Remedial Activity

During my 6-12 teacher-training, one of us students asked our teacher Margaret Stephenson what to do if a child was wasting a lot of time, or for some other reason just not getting anything accomplished. She told us that, only as a remedial technique, one could suggest that the child make a journal for a few days of just what they did during the day, looking at the clock and recording the beginning and ending time of the work. This would help the child discover where the problem lay, so the teacher didn't have to micro-manage the child.

A Problem with Daily Journals

Later, when I was working as a consultant for a Montessori school, I observed students writing in a journal every day. Even if they were not having to record the clock time, they were being required to record their work every day, from the very first day that they entered the elementary class. I will let a child speak about this.

Here is a piece of writing from a child visiting from a Montessori class where he was required to write in a journal every day. It is clear that he was writing in cursive but because he was required to write so much he never had the opportunity to back up, slow down, and learn to write in a way that he enjoyed, where he could concentrate deeply and be proud of his work. In case you cannot read it, this is what he wrote (his spelling):

I hate riting fast and slopily

I hate riting

I hate riting

I hate riting

I hate riting

I love carrots.
I hate riting
Sloppily
Sloppily
Sloppily
— Montessori and Mindfulness (page 76)

What is Repeated Over and Over is Learned

Years ago, having attended lectures at the annual Suzuki music conference in San Francisco, and then at the Suzuki training center in Japan, I took it upon myself to teach our son the first book of Suzuki piano. I was very impressed by the way every movement was analyzed, broken down into minute steps that a child could easily master, and be inspired to want to learn more. It was very much like Montessori. For my own classical piano training the system was basically to just repeat and repeat until one had learned the piece. I had good teachers but there was not this kind of attention to detail. It was commonly thought that after a number of years of this method some students would discover that they had natural talent and others did not. The training center in Japan is called Suzuki Talent Education because the belief is that talent can be learned.

A student having this kind of authentic training is taught to play beautifully from the very beginning, even if it only means sitting at the piano with good posture, holding the hands in the perfect position, and carefully playing three notes.

When a student is encouraged to play a piece on the piano badly, hoping for some miracle of improvement, the brain assumes that this is the correct way. When a student is asked to write without having detailed lessons on how to write beautifully the brain assumes that this is the correct way. Then bad, messy, illegible writing is learned, and in both cases, it is very difficult to relearn, to unlearn.

Children feel very good about themselves and tend to write far more when they have been taught beautiful handwriting. Giving a child a new alphabet and a different kind of writing utensil often does wonders to inspire writing. The Italic script is very beautiful and a link between cursive and print. I have seen a child's cursive writing improve dramatically as he casually worked through a set of Italic workbooks over a period of months.

Brain research today helps us understand the process of learning, of making a new skill a habit. It is important to understand this when helping a child learn to write. The cortex is used in learning to write. The formation of each letter activates a specific set of neurons in the brain. As the formation of a letter is repeated over and over gradually it is "learned," and the neurons needed to form letters are now those in the lower part of the brain, the habit area controlling activities that have become automatic. At this point the neurons in the brain that were previously activated in the cortex shrink and prepare for new challenges, new skills to be learned.

Think about this. Each time a child writes a letter badly, repeating it over and over, the ugly way of writing this letter become more and more "learned" and eventually is related to the lower part of the brain. It will be very difficult for him to ever write that letter beautifully.

When I learned this, I understood why my teacher Margaret Stephenson said to never ask a child to write anything that he cannot write beautifully. And do not criticize ugly writing because after all it is the adult that allowed ugly writing to develop. Instead she suggested that at this time, the beginning of the 6-12 stage of development, we introduce a new script. If the child had learned print before this, introduce cursive. If he has learned cursive, introduce italics. This helps him slow down and work carefully on the formation of letters. She suggested that we introduce colored inks to make the process even more careful with the results being even more beautiful. I followed her advice, even giving beautifully written short poems for the child to copy, and to decorate the margins with these same colored inks.

One day an 8-year old who had been asked to write every day in a journal in his previous school, asked me quietly if I would help him learn to write "better." He was very interesting to talk to, and had original ideas on every subject, and loved to share them. But he could only do this verbally because he said he hated to write. I gave him a lined piece of paper and at the beginning of the first line wrote, as slowly and beautifully as possible, a cursive letter. I asked him to fill the line with that letter as slowly as I had done. When he was finished together we studied each letter he had written, discussing each in detail. "Had it touched the base line? Had it reached the top line? What do we think of the slope? And the width of the loops?" Then I asked him to circle the letter that he decided was closest to the model. After several letters, I asked if he would like to write some words using these letters, or a sentence. I should not have done that; it was too early. His face fell and he said, "I can't and I hate to write ugly!" He was a perfect example of someone who had, because he was required to write when he had not been taught to write beautifully, learned well how to write badly, and he now had to completely rewire parts of his brain. Not an easy task.

— Child of the World: Montessori, Global Education for Age 3-12+ (page 111)

After observing in several elementary classes where looking at a clock and recording one's work throughout the day was standard practice, I tried it myself at home for three days. I urge anyone who is asking students to do this to try it themselves.

I discussed this with my friend neuroscientist Adele Diamond who knows a lot about Montessori. I said, "When I finish a task during a work day to look at the clock and record the time, as children are sometimes asked to do, it was like being forced to move to a part of my brain where no real concentration is happening, where connections could not be made, and where nothing was discovered or created."

Her reply? "I agree. You want to be in the moment. Once you are observing yourself being in the moment, you are no longer in the moment."

As she had told us in keynote speech at the Annual General Meeting of The Association Montessori International in Amsterdam in 2010:

In order to create, one must be in the moment and be allowed to stay there.

— Montessori and Mindfulness (page 59)

I learned, during a school consultation, that one of the ways students were keeping track of their work was to make a list, at the end of the day, of all of the work they had accomplished that day. So, of course, the first thing I did after returning home was to try this myself for a few days. I wanted to know what this felt like. From the first day on, it was just as painful for me as when I experimented with recording work—along with the time of beginning and ending a project—during a day.

At the end of a work day at home, in my office and art studio—even though I will have made notes to myself throughout the day for what to do in the future—I am in the moment, and ready to move on; my mind is free to welcome my husband home, to go for a walk or play the piano, to begin working on dinner. Having to step out of this flow experience, to make a list of what I had done during the day, was very much an intrusion of being in the moment and enjoying "now."

Even though I might offer the possibility of doing this to an interested student, I would certainly not require it were I teaching in an elementary class today.

Students' Unique Great Work

Standard traditional education today tends to value language and math over other subjects. These are easy to teach, grade, and compare. Human beings have many ways of learning, and many other skills that are valuable to society. During a class with Dr. Howard Gardner at the Harvard Graduate School of Education, we were tasked to work together in small groups to present a common school lesson using more than one of the "intelligences" or learning styles: Word Smart (linguistic intelligence); Math Smart (numerical/reasoning/logic intelligence); Physical Smart (kinesthetic or movement intelligence); Music Smart (musical intelligence); People Smart (interpersonal intelligence); Self Smart (intrapersonal intelligence).

Our group created a dance to represent the formation of a specific cell. Then we all presented our mixed-intelligences lessons to the rest of the class.

Later, when visiting the Montessori elementary class of a colleague, I witnessed a dance, created by the students—music, costumes, painted background, even written and decorated programs for the audience—to present photosynthesis in a leaf. I think this kind of creation represents the highest form of Montessori education at this age.

Over the years it has been a joy to witness what elementary students can come up with in this kind of freedom and encouragement.

The two boys below became very interested in plant classification. The materials for this work allow one to fit one classification inside the next in a kind of "Chinese box" configuration of smaller and smaller envelopes or folders: *Kingdom Plantae*, then *division*, then *class*, *order*, and *family*. At the same time, similar materials are used to construct a tree of life of plants. These two boys wanted to reach beyond what I had made for the class, to research and create their own tree of the life of plants. Above you can see them, so proud of their work, and below a detail of the labeled circles of the tree.

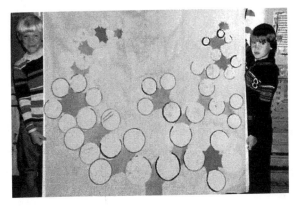

What was particularly interesting was that there was no consideration of what would happen to a creation, that took weeks of work, when it was finished. Their goal had nothing to do with ownership of the finished product. The goal was to learn, to explore and satisfy curiosity, to work together, to concentrate, all of the goals one hopes for.

> The secret of success is found to lie in the right use of imagination in awakening interest, and the stimulation of seeds of interest already sown by attractive literary and pictorial material, but all correlated to a central idea, of greatly ennobling inspiration – the Cosmic Plan in which all, consciously or unconsciously, serve the Great Purpose of Life.
> — Montessori, *To Educate the Human Potential*

BECOMING A YOUNG ADULT

The main focus of this book is, as is says on the cover, observation and recordkeeping for the Montessori primary and elementary class, but in this last chapter I share a few observations, experiences, and quotes about what happens after age twelve.

Today there is a conflict between what human beings are programmed to do during adolescence, and what is required by modern society. Age 12-18 has forever been the time when a human enters the first stage of adulthood, with genetic programing to: have adventures, fall in love, write poetry and engage in other areas of the creative arts, create and nurture a family, build and run a home and a village or town, explore society and morality, play an active and responsible and respected role in a society. Modern life requires putting all of these natural instincts on hold, focusing mainly on academics. Such a conflict can cause frustration and stress.

Inspired by visiting German land schools, Landerziehungsheime, in the 1920s Montessori came to believe that a boarding school, where adolescents carry out real work running a farm, a store, and a small hotel for visitors, would create the optimal environment for the adolescent. This was seen as a place that supported the development of bodies as well as the intellect and sense of social order. Hershey Montessori Erdkinder, in Ohio, United States, was founded in 2000 and since that time Erdkinders have been developed in many other countries, including Africa, Australia, Mexico, Sweden, Germany, recently the Czech Republic.

However, the percentage of students who have the opportunity to live on an Erdkinder is tiny. Montessori middle and high schools in cities around the world are doing their best to provide part-time farm school

*experiences, and to adapt the needs of city life to the needs
of the young adult.*

*This last chapter offers a brief overview of the needs
at this age. With such an understanding, it is hoped that
parents, and teachers in Montessori and other schools,
will have more of an understanding of young adults, and
come up with creative ways to support their needs in
school and at home,*

*Life in the open air, in the sunshine, and a diet high
in nutritional content coming from the produce of
neighboring fields improve the physical health, while the
calm surroundings, the silence, the wonders of nature
satisfy the need of the adolescent mind for reflection and
meditation. Work on the land is an introduction both to
nature and to civilization and gives a limitless field for
scientific and historic studies. If the produce can be used
commercially this brings in the fundamental mechanism
of society, that of production and exchange, on which
economic life is based. This means that there is an
opportunity to learn both academically and through actual
experience what are the elements of social life. We have
called these children the "Erdkinder" because they are
learning about civilization through its origin in
agriculture. They are the "land-children."*

– Montessori, *From Childhood to Adolescence*

The Young Adult, Age 12-18

Montessori considered the first twelve years the beginning and
culmination of childhood, the second twelve years the beginning and
culmination of becoming a young adult.

Academics are often the main consideration now as one prepares for university or other avenues of preparation for adult life. But moral, physical, and emotional considerations are at least as important.

Today there is an AMI teacher-training course for the age 12-18 level that provides skilled professionals, or any anyone interested in human development at this age, the training to understand and support the young adult following Montessori principles.

The Adult as Model

> The teachers must have the greatest respect for the young personality, realizing that in the soul of the adolescent great values are hidden, and that in the minds of these boys and girls there lies all our hope of future progress and the judgement of ourselves and our times.
> — Montessori, *From Childhood to Adolescence*

There is a saying that "love" is not just an emotion; it is an action. The same can be said for "respect". If we respect a child's ability to independently choose work, we show respect by supporting the choice. If we want to be the model for "treating one the way one would like to be treated" we must always keep in mind how we speak to our students at this age.

Parenting and Teaching

The expectations are different for the parent and the Montessori teachers. Daily life in the home can be very rushed, and busy. Each member has schedules and needs that are different from the others in the family. These needs cause conflicts, and no matter how hard a parent tries to maintain an attitude of calm and respect for the other members of the family, there will be problems! As I have said before, as we work to meet the need of the child, and young adult, we also must consider the needs of the adult, the parent, and not be too hard on ourselves. All parents are striving to do the best they can for their children,

I have all three levels of Montessori training, from birth through age twelve, and over fifty years of Montessori experience. When in the classroom I was able to be kind and calm and patient, to observe, discover, and support the needs of each of my students for thirty or forty hours a week.

But at home? There is so much to balance in the home, so many unexpected events and problems to deal with, that I have been known to be impatient, frustrated, and angry. My parents, who were excellent parents, were the same. Even though they were always trying to do their best for us they sometimes became impatient and lost their tempers.

My grandparents had more time, only spent special times with us, and it was much easier for them to be patient. I am the same with my grandchildren, and I imagine some of the readers know what I am talking about. With family visits, it is possible to set aside most other responsibilities and devote time to grandchildren when they visit. So, let us be easy on ourselves as we do our best, at home and in the classroom.

Voice and Words Matter

There is a saying in Montessori 0-3 practice, "The adult is the most important Montessori material."

It is the same for the adolescent years. Sometimes we do not even realize that our words and actions can make a huge difference in how we show respect for the adolescent.

I had a personal experience of this that I would like to share. It was during the time that I was a counselor for girls, ages 12-18, in a detention center in California. This was just before I discovered Montessori.

Some of the girls and I had gathered, informally, in the living room for "free time" before dinner. I was seated on one of the sofas with the girls talking about their school work, or any other subject brought up. A young priest, who was there to speak to any of the girls who would like to talk about religion with him, joined us. I noticed he had a foreign accent and so I asked him, "Where did you grow up?" By his response to my questions it was clear that he thought I was one of the girls.

His response was very kindly meant, but he raised his voice just a bit, and used an oversimplified vocabulary to deliver an oversimplified and patronizing explanation, something like, "I grew up on an island called Malta. Malta is far, far away from California in the middle of a sea."

His voice and his words were unexpectedly shocking to me, and it was clearly shocking to the girls. They were embarrassed for me and for the priest, and when I told him that I was a counselor for the girls, he was embarrassed about what he said and how he had said it.

This may sound like a small thing, but I hope it was as much a lesson in respect for everyone in the room, as it was for me. Here I share an example, quoting the book "*Montessori Homeschooling*" of how it helped me as a teacher throughout the years:

> As a school consultant, I often find myself talking
> about how to truly show respect to students. We of course
> know to respect concentration by not interrupting it, and

to respect a child's choice of work by not judging or preventing if it is suited to their stage of development; but there is more.

We are models first and foremost and our body language, our voice, our words, express how much we truly respect and believe in a student.

Dr. Silvana Montanaro, during our 0-3 Montessori teacher training, enlightened us all in this aspect of true respect when she modeled talking to an infant with the same pitch, vocabulary, and seriousness, as she would use in talking to any of us.

By 1993 I had been teaching and working with children from age two through high school for many years. I was approached by two Montessori teachers in Portland, Oregon who wanted to pick my brain about their elementary and middle-school teaching practice.

Maggie and Kathy and I spent several days together in our home. On the last day, we spoke about how to guide children while showing respect. I knew, as I heard them talk about their classes that they were speaking to students with a different voice than they would use in speaking to peers. I wanted to help them understand how being talked to in this way feels.

We were seated at a picnic table in our yard. I asked both teachers to stand next to each other on the deck against the wall of the house. Then I spoke to them the way my teachers might have spoken to me in traditional school when I was growing up, and unfortunately the way I still hear some Montessori teachers speak to students at times. They stood next to each other, waiting.

I stood next to the picnic table with my arms crossed in front of me and with a serious (teachery) expression on my face. But still using a polite voice I said:

We are going to walk down the hall. Please stand in line.

Stand still.

Kathy, put your hands by your side.

Maggie, no talking. Did you hear me?

I'll wait here until everyone is ready.

Maggie looked shocked, and then she slumped forward and called out, "Stop Susan, I get it!"

I asked them if they felt that I was respecting them.

Kathy replied, "It felt so belittling and controlling."

When I was writing this chapter of *Montessori Homeschooling* I reached out to Maggie and Kathy, both still Montessori teachers, to find out if there were things they had changed after our discussion about showing respect through our words. Here is what Kathy wrote:

> *"For me it changed my way of relating to students. I starting talking to them as I would another older person and trying to interest them in things the way I would another peer. I would say, "I read an interesting book about Lewis and Clark and was fascinated by . . ." And next thing the child was interested too. It helped me watch for and pull out their interests.*
>
> *It also changed the way of talking to students when they were being too loud, for example. I recall being out to dinner with my parents once and becoming loud and excited until finally a waitress came over and said, "Sorry but your table is being loud and that table said they are having a hard time hearing each other talk." Everyone laughed and we quieted down. The waitress didn't come over and say, "You are being too loud; you need to be quiet. Or you will have to separate. This is one warning..." Your example came to mind.*

I began to see how ridiculous it was to talk to people like that. If I said, "We are doing some work over here and can't hear each other because it is loud" the students would fix it without my saying anything else.

Yours was a life-shifting lesson for me. And has allowed me to have good relations with young people over the years.

— Montessori Homeschooling, One Family's Story
(page 186)

Here is another example. Years ago, I was studying French at *Alliance Française* in Paris. Over lunch we students sometimes could visit with our teachers, laughing together at our attempts at rudimentary French. After lunch, we returned to the classroom. The teacher entered the room and closed the door and transformed into the boss who held all the knowledge, which would be forced on us according to her schedule and directions. I know this is tradition in many places but it is not the kind of education that makes a person feel respected, excited, and inspired to want to learn more.

This kind of "talking down" to a person is embarrassing to adults, and it should not be something that our adolescents are used to. I cringe when I hear even the nicest Montessori teachers speaking this way to children at any age. There is a better way.

Two Aspects of Montessori Education for Age 12-18

It is necessary to keep close to nature to assist it by responding to the special needs of development that are experienced at different ages and therefore to consider separately:

1 - The moral and physical care of the pupils
2 - The syllabus and methods of studies

Moral and Physical Care, Age 12 to 15

The first three years of childhood compared to the first three years of adulthood

There are several similarities between birth to three and age twelve to fifteen.

Here are just some examples:

(1) Growth is rapid and it is difficult for parents to keep up with the changes. When an infant begins to crawl, there are two impulses; one is to be independent and strike out on one's own, and the other is to return to the parent for security. It is the same for adolescents. One moment they feel like capable adults, able to strike out on their own and make the correct decisions about life, and the next moment return to the parents for a hug and encouragement.

(2) As the body grows the environment must change to keep up. The infant wants and needs to imitate those older people in the home, to be given the opportunity to do real work such as dusting, raking leaves, setting the table, whatever is observed in the home. The young adult also needs to be trusted to do real, important, and valuable work, work that contributes to the social group, the family, or the class.

(3) The response by others, to these rapid changes, can be confusing to the child and young adult. The parents, seeing the young adult daily, might not notice the gradual changes, but a grandparent or a family friend, who might not see this person often, can be confused. They have returned expecting the same child they interacted with on the last visit, but now they find a completely different person. The young child is more independent and capable and wants to be respected as such. The young adult might be taller, thinner, have body hair and a changed voice, seeming more like an adult, and the visitor is confused about how to communicate. Just at the time when the adolescent might feel insecure about their changing body, this can be an unwelcome confusion.

(4) And finally, because of the rapid physical changes, in order to maintain physical, mental, and emotional health, the need for sleep and healthy food is very important in both of these periods of life.

No young adult wants to be told what to eat. But in a situation where students study the composition of soil, compost food wastes, plant and grow their own food, harvest, and cook meals, then they learn, from providing the nutritional needs of plants and animals, that meeting their own needs are just as important.

There is also a need to support the young adult's changing sleep needs. At this age, there is a strong need for self-exploration and discussing the meaning of life, one's purpose and potential, relationship, and more, with peers. They need time and support for figuring out "who" they are, "what" they are good for, "how" they might be valuable members of society in the future, and to talk about a natural developing love for another person. But when the day is filled up with classes, sports, extra-curricular activities, meals, and homework, this kind of exploration with peers can often only take place late at night, causing oversleeping and a vicious cycle.

Again, this sleep need is easier to support in an Erdkinder, but when we understand these adolescent needs, the family and urban Montessori school teachers can work together to support the young adult.

Moral and Physical Care, Age 15 to 18

If the physical, moral, and emotional needs have been met in the first three years of adolescence young adults will be more calm, self-aware, and responsible. The hormones, the bodies, are still changing, there is more interest in sexuality, but if the satisfaction with themselves is solid, and they are aware of, and in charge of, correct sleep and food, this period will be more successful.

This is the age when it is natural to be interested in babies and parenting. It is often the case that Montessori 0-3 teachers offer to young adults at this age, or even earlier, timelines to explain menstruation, pregnancy, and child rearing. Here are some quotes from the teacher, and some of the students in a Montessori adolescent program in the United States. Not having a Montessori 0-3 to meet with the students, they used the book *The Joyful Child: Montessori, Global Wisdom for Birth to Three* as a text in a human development course:

> Teacher: The Joyful Child *adds so much to our Human Development class. Its use brings alive the imaginative challenge of thinking about parenting, and it guides adolescents to think kindly about themselves and others.*

> Students: *I understand about being a parent better; I feel prepared to be a father.*

> *I saw how hard it is to be a parent. There is so much to keep in mind.*

> *I look at children differently now. Instead of wondering why they are doing something (like crying), I*

wonder what they are doing – what does the crying communicate:

I am using some of what I have learned in my own life, with a young child I know. I now give him limited choices, and it helps his behaviour a lot.

It has changed the way I look at children. Now I want to understand them (before I was annoyed and dismissive).

The Syllabus and Methods of Studies, Age 12 to 15

Students who have been through the Montessori elementary program, have experienced a wide-ranging and connected overview of, and introduction to, all knowledge available to humans. They have developed the responsibility and time-management skills to both meet the standard requirements, and explore widely. These young adults will be ready to continue this kind of work at the middle and high school levels. They will be prepared to forge unique paths and take responsibility for their choices

This is not the time for academic demands! Since the physical and emotional needs are so great, there is little time for, or patience with, the kind of academic learning that requires a person to sit still and listen to someone talk, or to take seriously the idea that an adult knows more about what they should study and become curious about.

These young adults do not do well with pressure on academic learning now. Their bodies give a clear message at puberty that they are becoming adults. Sometimes it is thought that these young adults are intellectually weaker because of the physical and emotional needs taking precedence; but I think they are intellectually very strong when offered work that they think is valuable to them, and useful NOW. They are interested when their work is practical and connected to everyday life.

One of the reasons Montessori recommended the Erdkinder, or Earth Children, boarding school for this age is because parents find it difficult to adjust to the fact that their children are becoming adults. When one has been living in the same home with one's child for twelve years it is not easy to observe, less to understand, the stage of becoming an adult. Parents want their children to be safe, and happy, and to do well socially and in school. But with such rapid changes at this age, there can be many hurdles to overcome in the parent/child relationship.

Montessori's words concerning the program for the first three years of adolescence:

> The children have some time for study, but they are completely free to study what they like and the means to do so are given them.
> — Montessori, "Development and Education of the Adolescent Essay from Kodaikanal (from Communications, 2011/1-2, Journal of the Association Montessori International

The Syllabus and Methods of Studies, Age 15 - 18

For age fifteen to eighteen, when the rapid growth of adolescence is slowing, a more rigorous intellectual schedule can be attempted, combined with social work and apprenticeships in the adult world of work and professions. When there is the possibility of mixed age groups, from 12-18, these young adults will be the models, the teachers, for the younger. They will be well on their way to continued discovery of who they are, and be looking forward to being a contributing adult.

Apprenticeships have for thousands of years been a way for young adults to learn real-life practical skills, but today good laws, created to stop child-labor, make it difficult for the young adult to learn practical skills or to earn money through work. One of the most important lessons has to do with money, learning how much time and work is involved in earning money, and how to use it for meeting real needs. In an Erdkinder this can be possible because students are allowed to do real work whenever possible. But even in urban schools there can be possibilities for young adults to learn from others.

The goal of all of these efforts, individually and in community, is to give value, to *valorize*, the personality of the young adult.

Conclusion

To end this final chapter, here are a few more quotes that have inspired many people working with young adults. I hope you enjoy them.

> *The need that is so keenly felt for a reform of secondary schools concerns not only an educational, but also a human and social problem. Schools, as they are today, are adapted neither to the needs of adolescents nor to the times in which we live. Society has not only developed into a state of utmost complication and extreme contrasts, but it has now come to a crisis in which the peace of the world and civilization itself are threatened. More than to anything else it is due to the fact that the development of man himself has not kept pace with that of his external environment.*
>
> *But above all it is the education of adolescents that is important, because adolescence is the time when the child enters the state of adulthood and becomes a member of society. If puberty is, on the physical side, a transition from an infantile to an adult state, there is also, on the psychological side, a transition from the child to the adult who has to live in society. These two needs of the adolescent: for protection during the time of the difficult physical transition, and for an understanding of the society which one is about to enter to play a part as an*

*adult, give rise to two problems that are of equal
importance concerning education at this age.*

*The world is partly in a state of disintegration and
partly in a state of reconstruction . . . It is necessary that
the human personality be prepared for the unforeseen, not
only for the conditions that can be anticipated by prudence
and foresight . . . one must be strengthened in one's
principles by moral training and must also have practical
ability in order to face the difficulties of life. [Young
adults] with hands and no head, and with head and no
hands are equally out of place in the modern community.*
— Montessori, *From Childhood to Adolescence*

*My vision of the future is no longer of people taking exams and
proceeding on that certification from the secondary school to the
university, but of individuals passing from one stage of independence
to a higher, by means of their own activity, through their own effort
of will, which constitutes the inner evolution of the individual.*

—Montessori, *From Childhood to Adolescence*

More Information

Excellent articles having to do with Montessori programs for
adolescents are found in journals that have been published over the
years by NAMTA, The North American Montessori Teachers
Association. An online source for many of these articles is ERIC,
The Institute of Education Sciences. To see them, go to the main
ERIC website and search "NAMTA" and "adolescents":

https://eric.ed.gov

ABOUT THE AUTHOR

During the last fifty years the author has lived on three continents, traveled in over seventy countries, and carried out Montessori work in thirty of them. She has a unique perspective on the problems of human beings. She is convinced that, with the proper support for parents and other educators, there is a chance to support a generation ready and willing to take up challenges, and solve problems, in unforeseen ways.

A person's upbringing and education, in her opinion, must not be limited to considerations of an outdated academic recipe; it must instead focus on practical and spiritual approaches such as that of Montessori, approaches that have at their core methods that can reveal and support the very best instincts—balance, curiosity, love of work, and compassion for others. This is the true meaning of "education," a word that comes from the Latin *educere*, interpreted as revealing, or exposing to the outside, what we have discovered already exists in the human being.

Before discovering Montessori, Susan worked as a Latin tutor for high school students and a counselor for troubled youths in a California detention center, youths from both the most privileged families and the best schools, and those from the poorest and most destitute.

She has degrees in philosophy, world religions, and education, and has studied learning styles, or *multiple intelligences,* under Dr. Howard Gardner, at Harvard Graduate School of Education. Susan has earned three Association Montessori Internationale diplomas (ages 0-3, 3-6, 6-12), and has experience guiding children and young adults from birth through age eighteen. This excellent teacher training, and teaching experiences, provided ample preparation for her present work as a writer, consultant, speaker, and examiner for AMI teacher training courses.

Susan enjoys exploring the meaning of life and the potential of education for the future, with adults as much as with children and young adults. She is also an artist; her paintings and prints are found in homes and schools on six continents. For more about this work see her website and blog at www.susanart.net

OTHER BOOKS IN THIS SERIES

The Joyful Child:
Montessori, Global Wisdom for Birth to Three

Susan Stephenson's book truly reflects the spirit and purpose of Montessori in a way that makes the philosophy translatable to both new parents and veteran Montessorians. Susan's passion for the pedagogy, her extensive experience, and her world travels resonate as she explores the universal, emotional, and psychological depths that construct the child's development.

—Virginia McHugh, past Executive Director of The Association Montessori International USA (AMIUSA)

Child of the World:
Montessori, Global Education for Age 3-12+

This book explains the meaning of life, how you are supposed to live it. It would be helpful to other people my age. If the young person does not want to read the chapter, The Young Adult, Age 12-18, *then the parents should read it so they can help their son or daughter become a better person.*

—Ryan Alcock, Montessori student, age 13, Amsterdam

Stephenson's volume is a wonderful resource for parents seeking thoughtful, sound advice on raising well-grounded children in a chaotic world. Presenting Montessori principles in clear and eloquent prose, Stephenson's legacy will be a tremendous service to generations of parents to come.

—Angeline Lillard, PhD, professor of psychology, University of Virginia, author of *Montessori, The Science behind the Genius*

The Red Corolla, Montessori Cosmic Education (for age 3-6+)

Susan Mayclin Stephenson, Montessori trained 0-3, 3-6, 6-12, with experience at all levels, writes many practical books about Montessori education. Her book, The Red Corolla: Montessori Cosmic Education, *translated into many languages, has a section titled: The Work of the Child. In this section, she has a sub-section on Physics in which she shares how to do many science experiments. She describes how to set up the science experiments and gives presentations. This book is a wonderful resource for a primary teacher (3-6 year olds) all taken from Susan's primary training in London many years ago. The book also deals with other areas of science, e.g., botany, zoology, plus music, geography, art, history, etc. If 3-6-year-old children can experience as much as possible of these materials, they have created a lovely foundation for the Cosmic Education of the elementary years.*

—Judi Orion, Director of Pedagogy,
Association Montessori International (AMI)

What I like about this book is the possibility that it will give to teachers who have not learned in their training this way of presenting the various cultural areas—art, music, geography, biology, and physics—to young children. That is, how to offer it in such a way that the child freely chooses to absorb the materials. Scattered throughout the book is information on approaching various ages of children, not just the young one.

—Rita Zener, PhD, AMI 3-6 Montessori Teacher Trainer

The Universal Child, Guided by Nature

The Universal Child, *more than anything else I have read, helps me understand the value and potential of a Montessori education.*

—School administrator new to Montessori, USA

Simple, elegant, inspiring. Susan Stephenson carries Dr. Montessori's vision of education for peace forward with this lovely, simple book about what we can all recognize as universal in our make-up as human beings. Those things that ought to (and can) bring us to a place of great respect for children through positive, intelligent engagement with them the world over.

—Gioconda Bellonci, Montessori parent and teacher

Montessori and Mindfulness

The author has a deep and broad understanding of Montessori and life long experience with meditation. Supplemented by wonderful pictures and stories from worldwide travels, this book gives a sound portrayal of how mindfulness manifests in this most profound and wise approach to children's education. Many thanks!

—Angeline Lillard, PhD, Professor of Psychology, University of Virginia, author of *Montessori, The Science behind the Genius*

The author writes with such clarity and simplicity yet takes on the complexity of Montessori philosophy and contemporary thoughts on mindfulness with such grace and care. Her overall theme that personal fulfillment leads to care for others and for our environment echoes throughout each chapter and creates a wonderful symbiosis of Montessori thought and Mindfulness practices, with interestingly retold personal stories throughout. I really like the way Susan distills the essence of Montessori into such an accessible and inspiring book.

232

No Checkmate, Montessori Chess lessons for Age 3-90+

This book can tell you how to teach chess to any child in a Montessori way. But if you look past the chess, you can use this book as an insight to teach your child anything, using the Montessori method. The book introduces the game of chess using: grace and courtesy of handling the chess pieces, and the social aspect of the game; practical life— polishing/dusting the pieces, setting up the environment; language, using the three-period-lesson to learn the names of the pieces; mastering the game by building up one difficulty at a time. This is the essence of Montessori. If you are not interested in learning chess this book is still a gold mine of knowledge and insight into the Montessori method and how to offer any skill to a child. As always, this author welcomes you into the world of the child and how to help spark their interest.

—Joanne King, Montessori primary and elementary consultant, the Netherlands

If you are looking for a book that will help you to introduce the game of chess to your child—in a non-competitive, gradual, and fun way—you have found it! Deep respect and understanding of human development in its formative stages is a common denominator of all Ms. Stephenson's books. In No Checkmate, *you will find a conceptual framework of developmental characteristics along with a practical guidance in the form of preliminary games and activities, gradual introduction to the key rules of the game, and more. This book opened a new field of exploration and joy for me and my two daughters!*

—Dmitry Ostrovsky, father, philosopher,
Montessori elementary teacher, Israel and Russia

Montessori Homeschooling, One Family's Story

I highly recommend this book for Montessori teachers for ages 6-18 even more so because it reminds us that we offer keys to the world and a variety of ways for the child to explore it. As teachers, our vision is to lend an inspiration only until the child's own inspiration is lit and this book shows us how this can be done both through practical glimpses into the family's homeschooling days, as well as through the examples of the homeschooler's own journal reflections.

—Christine First, Montessori adolescent program, New Zealand

Our English department teachers read Montessori Homeschooling, One Family's Story *and then made a presentation to all the Middle and High School staff. The experience of their son was very impressive for the whole group of teachers. When students recognize the purpose and are a fundamental part of what they are learning, they are more likely to dig deeper, and find ways to learn about what is important and relevant to them. Teachers have come to nurture our students' desires and help them connect to their passions and interests.*

—The English teachers, Montessori Colegio Bilingue, Cali, Colombia

The author shares valuable, informative methods for how to teach and interact with children and teens. I am using the author's techniques at work with children from ages 7-18 with great success. Susan shares ways to treat children with respect and dignity and

234

receive that respect in return. Examples of how to achieve reciprocity are abundant in this gem of a book. This is a must-have for parents or people working with children of all ages and backgrounds.

—Kathy Wollenberg, counselor for young adults, USA

Each chapter describes one year of home schooling from kindergarten through twelfth grade. It is encyclopedic in detail and charmed with honesty about failures and successes. This is quite a span, with the right kind of limited stimulus exposed at the right ages and stages and leading to wider independence. It comes through with the widest scope at adolescence. They had four guidelines: keep the developmental stage in mind, prepare the environment and offer the work, observe to see if it is working, and lastly, adapt and "follow the child". This Montessori-inspired home-schooling centered in the family ended with Michael's acceptance at Brown University. It is more than a fairy tale; it is a triumph for all families to witness.

—David Kahn, Director Emeritus of NAMTA, North American Montessori Teachers Association, adolescent education speaker and consultant

Aid to Life, Montessori Beyond the Classroom

Chapters include:
Peru, A Montessori Class without Montessori Materials

A Montessori Q&A Newspaper Column
Nepal, Montessori for Forgotten Himalayan Children
Tibet, Braille without Borders
Tibetan Children's Villages
Montessori Teachers with the Dalai Lama in Sikkim
Russia, Montessori Help for Severe Disabilities
Morocco, An Orphanage, Village Schools, and a Garden
Thailand, Educateurs san Frontières (EsF)

Montessori at Home, 0-6
Montessori at Home, 6-18
A Grandparenting Literary Experience
Visiting a Montessori 3-6 class in London

It was Mr. Montessori's dream that his mother's, Dr Maria Montessori's, educational approach could be realized without being bound to a set of materials. He would be very pleased with this book. The author, Susan Stephenson, is fulfilling her dream in showing how all children can receive the Aid to Life that they need to develop their potential. It is very readable book, full of real life situations. The table of contents intriguing for finding just the answer one is looking for. This book will give confidence to parents who want Montessori for their child beyond the classroom.

—*Rita Zener, PhD, AMI Montessori Teacher Trainer*

This is a wonderful book about Montessori and how it is being used in many countries. We will be translating it into French.

—Victoria Barres, Association Montessori Internationale representative to UNESCO, The United Nations Educational, Scientific and Cultural Organization. Paris, France

Made in the USA
Columbia, SC
10 July 2022